DON'T BE A CRAB!

DON'T BE A CRAB!

A Practical Guide to Building
Strong, Joyful Relationships

HOOMAN MOTEVALLI

COPYRIGHT © 2023 HOOMAN MOTEVALLI
All rights reserved.

DON'T BE A CRAB!
A Practical Guide to Building Strong, Joyful Relationships

FIRST EDITION

ISBN   978-1-5445-4438-0 *Hardcover*
         978-1-5445-4437-3 *Paperback*
         978-1-5445-4436-6 *Ebook*

To all who love but still struggle to act on their passion in true service.

*To my Roommate, my closest friend, who
now supports me in serving others.*

To all who showed me how to love.

CONTENTS

	INTRODUCTION	9
1.	WHO'S CHIRPING IN MY HEAD?	21
2.	IT REALLY IS A CRAB!	33
3.	HELP! GET ME OUT OF THIS BUCKET!	45
4.	OMG! I FOUND A WAY OUT!	59
5.	SHOULD I LIFT MY FELLOW CRABS?	81
	CONCLUSION	99
	APPENDIX A: 10+1 EXERCISES	105
	APPENDIX B: 10+1 NOT TO DOS	117
	APPENDIX C: 10+1 FEARS	129
	ACKNOWLEDGMENTS	141
	ABOUT THE AUTHOR	143

INTRODUCTION

I HAD TALKED TO MY MOTHER ON THE PHONE THOUsands of times, but I had never answered a call and found her screaming. I immediately broke out in a cold sweat.

"Your father!" she finally managed to say between sobs.

In the weeks prior, my father had complained about feeling sick and discouraged, but I was away from my homeland at the time, so I couldn't help him. Plus, he always managed to visit medics by himself. When we spoke on the phone, I told him, "I'll be back in two weeks. We can find a solution if it continues."

"It may be too late by then," he replied.

As it turned out, he was right. He died the day after that conversation, and I was devastated. Consequently, a conversation started in my head that I couldn't stop. I blamed myself for not taking action. Even though I knew my mom had helped my dad in every way, I still told myself I should have called my friends and relatives who are doctors. I felt sick in the head, like something poisonous was pushing me to take responsibility for this horrible incident. But what action could I take? What could I do to change what had happened? Why couldn't I stop the conversation? How did I get so stuck?

Finally, I couldn't hold it all inside any longer. The pressure was too great. I decided to write down the conversation I was having with myself: *If I had done this… If I had talked to my father in a different way…* Then I shared what I wrote with a friend and asked him what he thought. I didn't tell him where these words came from.

"What's this rubbish?" he asked me. "This is bullshit. This guy should go see a therapist."

"That's from my mind," I said.

He was surprised. He saw me as someone who is mentally healthy, and he couldn't believe these confused thoughts were mine.

HUMAN CONFUSION FACTORIES

The situation with my father is a dramatic example, but we all engage in inner self-talk that leaves us confused and despairing. Why does this happen?

Think of how a factory works: materials go in, they are processed, and a product comes out. In a way, we humans function in the same input-process-output fashion:

- *Input*: In our daily lives, we soak up experiences, interactions, and information. By the time we are adults, we have received a lot of input from many different sources.
- *Process*: In response to these inputs, we talk to ourselves nonstop. This is how we process the incoming information. We discuss what we should or shouldn't do, what we should or shouldn't say, or what we should have said or not said in the past.

- *Output:* After we process, we react. We say things we regret. We blame and judge. We come off as crabby and ill-humored. We miss out on opportunities and hurt those we love. We don't feel happy, calm, or peaceful. At the extreme, we abuse others and even become killers.

As humanity has advanced, the inputs have increased. They have also become more complex and in many cases unhealthy. We are bombarded with messages from the internet, nonstop news feeds, and social media posts, as well as those transferred through our own personal history, genetics, and family. We get advice from the usual sources—parents, friends, partners, coworkers—as well as thousands if not millions of people online.

These inputs then enter a processing system—the mind—that is often faulty. This is where confusion comes in and causes us to deliver those negative, destructive outputs. We humans developed a brain mechanism that allows us to talk to ourselves to help us decide the best course of action. This mechanism has one goal: protection. It wants to keep us alive, first, and then keep us safe, calm, and at peace. There are two parties involved in this self-talk mechanism: ourselves and a voice that is part of us but not us. In his book *The Untethered Soul*, Michael Singer refers to this second voice as the Roommate. I like this description because it illustrates that the voice is closely connected to us, living in the same space.

The problem is that in its efforts to protect, our Roommate sometimes prompts us to act in ways that cause harm to ourselves and others. Based on our previous inputs, whether positive or negative, our Roommate advises us on how to respond to current inputs. Sometimes that advice is helpful, but more often it is not. Either way, we become confused because we can't tell if the advice is valid. We can't distinguish between the two voices in our head.

When you consider this input-process-output system, is it surprising that we humans suffer so much mentally? Doesn't it make sense that mental pain has increased in our modern world? While complexity has allowed for human advancements in medicine and technology, for example, it has also resulted in widespread negative outputs like child abuse, global warming, and terrorism, to name a few. Our one-on-one relationships suffer, and so does society as a whole.

So what can we do? Is there a solution?

Definitely! But you have to get to the root of the issue.

CONVERTING CONFUSION INTO CLARITY

Several months ago, I talked to a wise professor about my fatty liver.

"I have done many things to keep my liver clean," I told him. "I play a lot of sports and try my best to eat a healthy diet. Why is my liver still fatty?"

"Because you have never gone for real treatment," he responded. "You know there is a critical problem, so your mindset is to quickly find a remedy. In rushing, however, you don't go to the root."

The same is true when we see problems in our relationships or in society. We see the issues, and we want a quick fix. But this rarely works. We cannot use shortcuts to resolve conflicts with romantic partners, family members, colleagues, friends, or strangers, and political leaders cannot use them to resolve conflicts with each other. In fact, the problems often get worse when we do so because we make assumptions, then act in response. When our actions do not improve the situation, we become disappointed and angry and escalate the conflict.

Instead, we need to lay aside our assumptions and quick fixes.

We need to address the root: the *process* in the input-process-output system. Our nonstop internal conversations lie at the heart of the confusion that causes us to deliver hurtful outputs.

In this book, I offer a way to get to the root through the Converting Confusion into Clarity (CCC) training. We start by simply recognizing that this inner voice, our Roommate, exists, and that it causes confusion. Then we learn techniques for managing and finally training our Roommate so that it doesn't sabotage our relationships, ruin our reputation, and damage our mental health. As we each gain clarity in our individual processing system, we can start to improve society as a whole.

We discuss one level of the CCC training per chapter:

- Chapter 1: We'll start by considering one key question. *Is it there?* In other words, is there a conversation going on inside our head? In the CCC training, we call this Level 1: The Observer. Our goal at this stage is to become aware that we have a Roommate who engages us in nonstop conversation about the inputs we receive and the outputs we deliver.
- Chapter 2: Next we'll consider the importance of this conversation. Does it affect our lives and if so, how? In the CCC training, we call this Level 2: The Analyzer. We examine how our lives are impacted by this conversation. Our goal at this stage is to recognize that, yes, this conversation does affect our lives—and usually not in positive ways. This conversation and the confusion that results can destroy relationships, ruin reputations, and harm our mental health.
- Chapter 3: Next, the good news. In the CCC training, we call this Level 3: The Distinguisher. Our goal at this stage is to recognize the conversation as it's happening—not hours or days later when we're thinking about that awful thing we did. As we pause and listen to the voices in the midst of the

dialogue, we learn to distinguish between ourselves and our Roommate in real time.
- Chapter 4: Then we take the solution a step further. We don't want to simply notice when a conversation is happening. We want to be able to manage it so that it no longer keeps us stuck in unhealthy ways of thinking and acting. In the CCC training, we call this Level 4: The Manager.
- Chapter 5: After we've learned how to manage this conversation, we'll be in a position to train our inner voice with an eye toward service. This is an advanced level that might take years to achieve, but I want to share what is possible. We can change our inner self-talk so that it is predominantly focused on providing true service to others, to our world, and therefore to ourselves. In the CCC training, we call this Level 5: The Server.

I am currently developing a sixth level, The Alchemist, but it is still a work in progress. I am still learning how people with internal clarity can change our world for the better through a decentralized organization that empowers our planet and its inhabitants. I will save that level for a future book.

The best way to practice observing, analyzing, distinguishing, managing, and training ourselves to serve is through exercises and techniques. I share exercises at the end of each chapter, and then I've collected them all together in Appendix A. In Chapters 4 and 5, I present techniques for managing and training your self-talk and thus changing your outputs. I've gathered all of these "Not to Dos" in Appendix B.

When we start managing the conversation, we'll find several fears lying underneath our actions and reactions. In Chapter 4, we'll discuss the effects fears have on our lives. I've gathered a list of the most common fears in Appendix C.

Although I have laid out the levels in a linear way, the process is quite dynamic. As you learn to consider and then train your inner voice with new inputs, you will move back and forth through these levels. For instance, you may learn to recognize the voice on time in conversations with your partner, but then a new situation at work may arise, and you find yourself confused and reacting in ways you thought you had managed.

This happened to me when my father died and led to the training ideas you now hold in your hands.

LEARNING TO DISTINGUISH

I have been a soccer player since childhood, and I have watched many matches on television with my father and uncles. I have listened to them yell at the TV because someone missed an easy shot or kept the ball when he should have passed it to a teammate who was wide open. As a result, I started thinking about teamwork from a young age, and especially what factors can be barriers to teamwork. I noticed that confusion seems to be one of those barriers and that clarity opens the door to concentration and many other valuable skills.

In my thirties, I became a UEFA (Union of European Football Associations) soccer coach and noticed that the guys on the under-fourteen team had a much closer bond than the guys on the under-twenty-three team. After talking to the teams as a whole and privately with many players, I started figuring out why: the younger players had clearer heads. They didn't have the same internal conversation going on. They didn't blame their teammates as much or complain about coaches' decisions. The younger players hadn't yet learned the tricks that older players used on the manager, the coach, and their teammates.

I also realized that the players on the teams that were more cohesive had the same capabilities as the players on the other teams. They all had the same range of skills, so that wasn't the reason one team played better than the other.

When I competed in Kung Fu, I witnessed the same phenomenon on an individual level. In a field of competitors with basically the same capabilities, the factor that made a difference was having a clear mind.

I've since learned that the conversations in our head create barriers to teamwork, success, and personal growth in business and in life. After I finished my bachelor's and master's degrees, I entered the IT world of business. In many cases, I became the team trainer because I was able to find out what was really going on inside my colleagues' heads.

Then, in 2015, my father died unexpectedly, and I was faced with the confusion in my own mind.

Although that wasn't the first time I observed the conversation going on inside my head, it was the most obvious example of how important it is to be an observer. Writing down my thoughts and looking at them on the page made it so clear that there was a powerful, repetitive mechanism at work, something that was causing me to be unsettled and confused.

After that experience, I started researching this idea of an inner conversation. I found that several people had discussed it, in particular Michael Singer. He said that this conversation involves two parties—a speaker and a listener—and that the speaker is part of us, but it is not us.

This immediately made sense. I started working on managing this conversation in my own head. I realized how I reacted to these conversations with blaming and judging, among other things, and how it negatively impacted my relationships as a result. After a while, colleagues noticed that I no longer joined them in blaming this or that person. Family members noticed

I didn't react like I used to. Soon, I was informally sharing with workmates, family, and friends what I was learning about managing my inner voice.

After about two years of working on myself and informally sharing with others, managers began asking me to bring my ideas into more formal training for their teams. What started with groups of five people soon turned into training sessions with fifty or more. Then in 2019, I was asked to share on some college campuses and in other big group settings, and I have since formalized the training as the Converting Confusion into Clarity training you are now reading about.

DON'T BE A CRAB!

As the story goes, crabs display interesting behavior when they are placed in a bucket. If one crab tries to escape by crawling up the side, another will reach up and pull it back down.

If that same crab is placed in a bucket by itself, it can easily climb out. But in a bucket with other crabs, it is pulled back down every time.

What is happening here?

Psychologists now refer to this phenomenon as crab mentality. Think of the world as a bucket. We humans are the crabs inside. In the workplace and in our families and friend circles, we often see someone trying to advance or compete with our position, rank, or earning. What happens? Out of selfishness or jealousy, we sometimes pull that ambitious "crab" back down. We may pretend to be happy for him but try to prevent his progress. We may cut him down with our words and actions. In many ways, we attempt to keep him from progressing.

In addition, our Roommate acts like a crab toward *us*. Through the constant conversation and the confusion that results, our Roommate keeps us from moving forward. It supposedly protects us, but in reality, it often prevents our mental, emotional, and relational progress. It acts just like the crab in the bucket, pulling down its mate.

Although we cannot remove our Roommate, we can learn to decrease the confusion. We can learn to manage the way it claws at our brain and prevents us from progressing in our relationships, careers, and development as humans. We can get ourselves unstuck.

Many self-help books and trainers tell us to become a better version of ourselves—more honest, empathetic, and kind. They also ask us to "be ourselves" instead of pretending to be something or someone we're not. The problem is that they often don't share a practical way to do so. This book bridges that gap and offers a way to real change.

Though the training levels are easy to understand, the process of going through them will probably take you out of your comfort zone. When you write down your inner conversations and then read them, you will likely feel distressed. However, if you don't write them down, you won't be able to change.

But, if you are willing to feel a little uncomfortable, the transformations will be unbelievably valuable. Your relationships will become robust and joyful.

Are you ready to learn how? Let's start with discovering how to observe your inner voice.

OVERVIEW OF KEY TAKEAWAYS

This CCC training is dynamic. You will continue applying the key lesson from Level 1, for example, after you move on to Level 2 and beyond. Becoming proficient at observing, analyzing, distinguishing, and managing the conversation, as well as training your inner voice so that you can better serve others, takes time and practice.

Here's a quick glimpse of the key takeaway from each level:

- **Level 1: The Observer.** You will succeed in observing the conversations running in your mind most of the time.
- **Level 2: The Analyzer.** You will be able to analyze the internal chats to determine how they impact your relationships, reputation, and mental health.
- **Level 3: The Distinguisher.** You will be able to distinguish the roles in your internal conversations: the listener and decision-maker (you), and the speaker or inner voice (part of you, but not you).
- **Level 4: The Manager.** You will succeed in managing your inner voice so that you make better decisions in your relationships and in general.
- **Level 5: The Server.** You will be in a position to truly serve others because you have learned to train your inner voice.

Chapter 1

WHO'S CHIRPING IN MY HEAD?

A COUPLE OF YEARS AGO, AS MY FRIEND AND I RODE the metro, we noticed that almost every passenger was staring at their smartphone. "How much time do people spend on social media?" he asked me.

"I'm not sure," I replied. "I'm not a social media guy. Ask someone who uses those channels daily."

A few weeks later, I attended a gathering with the same friend. He made the same observation about people being on their smartphones and asked me the same question. "Like I said, I'm not a social media guy," I replied.

This time, however, my sister was standing right next to me. She turned and said, "But you like all of my posts and sometimes add some comments too! So, do you read them or not?"

"Yes, I read them!"

"Well, then maybe you are a social media guy," she said with a smile.

For the next few weeks, I thought about this conversation,

and I even talked to myself about it: *Am I a social media guy? I don't really spend that much time on Twitter and Instagram, do I?*

Then I used a tool on my smartphone that creates a report of time spent on social media. When I read the first month's report, I was shocked. I thought something was wrong, so the next month I kept track on my own and then compared it with the report.

It turns out the report was completely right. I was spending sixty to one hundred hours each month reading and commenting on posts from my favorite channels. I *was* a social media guy, even though I had been telling myself I wasn't.

After I made this discovery, I started thinking about why and how I had developed this wrong opinion of myself. *Was I talking to myself and telling myself stories? Was I pretending to look wise or intellectual? Why did I need to be seen as someone I'm not?*

Then I started wondering, *How much do we all talk to ourselves every day about different circumstances and events? Do we make a lot of faulty presumptions when we talk to ourselves? Is there a way to measure how much we talk to ourselves?*

This chapter explores these questions. It will help you become aware of the frequent conversations going on inside your head. It will also help you start noticing who is involved in those dialogues, and what role they play. As you'll see, one of these voices does a lot of talking or "chirping," just like a crab. Becoming an observer of these inner discussions is the goal of this first training level.

OBSERVING INTERNAL DIALOGUE

For several weeks after I realized I was a social media guy, I paid attention to how much I talked to myself. I also asked several relatives, colleagues, and friends to participate in an exercise to observe how much they talked to themselves, and to look at the nature of those conversations.

Seven people—five men and two women—agreed to participate in this month-long exercise I call Talk Check. There were three rules:

1. Keep track of how often you talk to yourself.
2. When you notice a conversation going on inside your head, try to stop it.
3. When you can't stop it, write it down word for word—including the words you use to try to stop the conversation.

Every Friday, the participants turned in a report that included these written conversations, as well as personal reflections and conclusions about the experience. Here is what we found.

RESULTS

One thing that became immediately apparent was that everyone talked to themselves. A lot. It also became clear that every single person had a hard time stopping the conversation once it started. For example, here's an excerpt from one person's report (the three dots indicate a pause or gap in the conversation):

> Why did my father say that? Why does he bother me? Oh, stop it... Yes, he does that intentionally. Oh, no! If it is intentional, why has he looked after and cared for me all the years? Stop it! Shut up... Anyway, he is one of the worst fathers ever. Why do I love him sometimes? Just stop it! Enough!!! He did that to me, yes! He did. I will never forget it. When he dies? No No. My God! What am I saying?

Before starting this exercise, participants thought they would be able to control the conversation. They thought it would be more challenging than commanding themselves to raise their hand or jump up and down, but they still thought it would be possible. They soon realized this was not the case. Instead, they found that conversations started without them making an intentional decision to do so. In addition, every single person realized that in most situations, they could not stop the conversation once it started. Instead, they tended to continue or restart it, again and again, until they became exhausted.

These realizations left everyone confused. Why couldn't they stop the conversation? How could these dialogues start without them intending to? And who or what was talking to them? Prior to this exercise, most people knew they talked to themselves, but they saw it as a monologue, not a dialogue. Now they wondered who else was participating in the chats.

Is there something else in our mind? If so, who or what is it? Is that something us, or is it only part of us?

SURPRISES

Each week we reviewed the reports, and there were a few surprises. For example, the two women had a harder time sharing with the group, perhaps because they were outnumbered by the men. In addition, one of the men refused to read any of his conversations because they involved his biggest secrets.

The best surprise was how the participants' lives changed as a result of the exercise. After one month of writing these conversations, without any other exercises or practice, all seven individuals said they were more lighthearted. They found humor in how they spoke to themselves and realized how often they talked to themselves about things that really weren't important.

As a result, their interactions with others changed. They became better listeners and reacted less often, which people noticed. The friends of one participant asked why he seemed so refreshed.

Are you intrigued by what you've read so far? Have you ever paid attention to how much you talk to yourself? I invite you to participate in the exercise just described so you become aware of your self-talk. Keep it simple. Find a fresh notebook, and start writing down your internal conversations whenever you have a chance. If you are more comfortable using Google Drive or something similar, then do that. The important part is to simply notice what is going on in your mind and write it down. Then you'll be ready to look more closely at one participant in that conversation.

WHO OR WHAT IS TALKING TO YOU?

After you write down your inner conversations for a few weeks, ask yourself, "Is it there?" That is, "Is there another voice besides my own participating in the dialogue?"

Like the seven participants mentioned earlier, you will probably say, "Yes, there is something talking to me. I cannot control it. It starts talking without my intention."

If you agree that something is there, the next question is, "Who or what is it?" Scientifically speaking, this inner voice or internal dialogue results from brain mechanisms that cause us to "hear" ourselves talk inside our head, even though we don't actually make sounds. Researchers have found that Broca's area and Wernicke's area, in particular, are both active when we hear voices.[1]

---

1   Kristeen Cherney, "Everything to Know about Your Internal Monologue," Healthline, last updated April 10, 2023, https://www.healthline.com/health/mental-health/internal-monologue; "Voices and the Brain," Understanding Voices, accessed April 19, 2023, https://understandingvoices.com/exploring-voices/why-do-people-hear-voices/voices-and-the-brain/.

I like to think of this inner voice as our Roommate—something that lives with us, is very close to us, is built into us, but is ultimately not us; it is only one part of us.

Think back to the earlier Talk Check exercise. Who did most of the talking in the example presented? The Roommate. Who did most of the listening? The participant, except when she tried to stop her Roommate from speaking. When you start writing out these conversations, you will likely find the same to be true. It is not easy to control the Roommate once it starts talking, but we can learn to manage it, as you will see.

HOW DOES YOUR ROOMMATE APPEAR?

Imagine you are relaxing on your back porch, sipping a cup of hot coffee on a beautiful spring morning. Nothing is bothering you. You are simply savoring your coffee and enjoying the light breeze. Suddenly, the sight of the tree swaying reminds you of a romantic memory, a time when you and your partner enjoyed a few days away. Then you remember that during a lovely dinner, your partner started discussing financial matters when you had agreed to remain present and focused on your relationship, not the problems at home. Your Roommate then begins a conversation involving this data from various layers of your brain's archives. Without your agreement, your Roommate has pulled you from this relaxing, pleasant experience and driven you into a dialogue that leaves you feeling unsettled.

Now imagine you are sitting in front of your computer, working on a tech report. You're trying to remember a technical part of your project so that you can add the details to your write-up. In that moment of intentional thinking, your Roommate appears and starts talking to you. You remember the last time you discussed the same tech problem with your colleague. After he resolved the issue, he tried to humiliate you and asked you to work harder. Again in the present moment, you unexpectedly feel unhappy and enraged.

Is there a difference in the way the inner conversation proceeds after the Roommate appears? Not really. It doesn't matter that in the first case, a thought randomly came to mind during a relaxed state, and in the other, you intentionally started thinking about a mathematical subject. In every situation, the Roommate appears, and the conversation proceeds from there. Our inner voice most often takes the role of speaker, but sometimes it can seem like it is both speaker and listener. That's why we think there is a monologue, not a dialogue, going on inside our head. As we learn to observe the conversation, however, we will see more clearly that there are two voices involved, and we most often take the role of listener.

What else can we say about this Roommate? Where does it find data to bring to the conversation, and how does it speak to us? Based on my work with many trainees, I've come up with the following characteristics:

- Our Roommate, as part of the mechanism in our brain, receives input from everything around us: news, media, relationships, childhood memories, and even our own behaviors and responses. And it gathers this data much more quickly than you might expect. You might not even remember the bits of a past conversation that your Roommate has collected.
- In any given situation or interaction, our Roommate brings these inputs into the self-chat very quickly, which means it can rapidly take control of the conversation.
- When it starts speaking, our Roommate often plays mind games using data from our background, genetic makeup,

and history. For years, and sometimes decades, our parents, grandparents, and teachers have transmitted information from their own inner conversations, which they received from their ancestors. Our Roommate uses this data to convince us to act in ways that supposedly protect us.

- As the speaker and/or listener in these inner conversations, our Roommate can take the form of a kind parent, lovely friend, wise mentor, strong guard, or loyal servant. On the other hand, it can appear as a nonstop analyst and critic, feeder of evil thoughts, hate dispenser, malicious agitator, and even a potential killer. In less than a minute, it can bring into the self-talk a dispute from a movie you recently watched and a conflict you witnessed two decades ago, and advise you on the current situation involving a family argument. It happens so quickly that you don't distinguish this advising voice from your own, and you don't check on the validity of its suggestion.
- The Roommate speaks clearly and fluently to *everyone* inside in their heads, even people who are deaf or who stutter when they speak aloud. We all have the brain mechanism that allows us to talk to ourselves, so we are all susceptible to the effects of this conversation.
- Our Roommate speaks quickly, at a rate of three to four thousand words a minute. Compare that with a professional speaker, who averages four to six thousand words *an hour*. That means we can move from hearing the first word to the hundredth or thousandth without even realizing it.[2]

---

2 Ethan Kross, *Chatter: The Voice in Our Head, Why It Matters, and How to Harness It* (New York: Crown, 2021).

As you will see in Chapter 2, many of these characteristics contribute to the confusion caused by our Roommate. The speed at which it engages and feeds us information, the games it plays, the varying forms it takes—all of these influence the processing in our mind and outputs that follow.

These attributes also make it harder to remember that our Roommate is part of us but not wholly us. It is only one side of the conversation. That said, if we don't learn to distinguish this inner voice from ourselves, we will never be able to manage it. In Chapter 3, we'll talk more about how to make this distinction.

WHAT IS THE ROOMMATE'S FUNCTION?

In 1943, Abraham Maslow proposed the idea that human motivation stems from felt needs, which he represented as a hierarchy from basic to transcendent:[3]

- Physiological: air, water, food, shelter, sleep, clothing
- Safety: personal security, employment, health, property
- Love and belonging: friendship, intimacy, family, connection
- Esteem: respect, status, recognition, freedom
- Self-actualization: a desire to become the most one can be

According to Maslow, we are always facing the next need or problem. Once one need is met, we immediately think about solving the next. As a result, we live with an underlying feeling of being in nonstop danger that leads the inner voice mechanism to be constantly on guard. Because our Roommate is

---

[3] Saul Mcleod, "Maslow's Hierarchy of Needs," Simply Psychology, last updated March 21, 2023, https://www.simplypsychology.org/maslow.html.

always on the lookout for threats to our well-being, it is inclined toward negative conversations.

The Roommate's goal is to keep us safe, to bring us back to the okay situation. Your state of being "okay" will not be the same as another person's, and that's fine. Your Roommate is only concerned with getting *you* back to *your* okay situation—that place where you are at peace, relaxed, and feeling safe.

In its efforts to protect us, however, our Roommate can cause us to act in ways that are actually harmful to our mental and emotional well-being. Maria, one of the female participants in the earlier exercise, was hurt by her male partner.[4] As a result, her inner voice highly recommended that it was safer to stay away from guys because that would protect her from being taken advantage of. Maria agreed with her Roommate because for four years after the adverse event, she didn't stay away from guys, and she was miserable. Then, for the next several years, she listened to her Roommate. She avoided relationships, and she was much happier.

Because Maria saw "proof" that her Roommate was right, she had a hard time seeing the problem her inner voice was causing. She developed a binary perspective about men: a man is bad (A man will treat me poorly. Even if he is kind at first, he will ultimately be unkind.) or he is ideal (A perfect man may find me in the future.) Even though she believed the perfect man might be out there, she avoided all men in the meantime because she believed they couldn't be trusted. The truth is, no one is perfect. We all have positive and negative qualities. Believing this all-or-nothing lie was her mind's way of keeping her safe, but it made Maria mentally sick. Her needs for belonging and connection with a romantic partner were not

---

4   In many of the stories in this book, names have been changed to protect people's privacy.

satisfied because she kept pushing men away, so she remained discouraged, even though she initially felt happier by avoiding relationships.

Can we leave needs unmet and still be healthy? No. And sometimes, it's our crabby Roommate who keeps us from having those needs met.

IMPORTANCE OF YOUR ROOMMATE

Do you see that your Roommate exists? Do you see that it is something that is part of you, but not actually you? This understanding is the first step toward addressing the confusion that results from your inner conversation.

As you can see from Maria's story, this Roommate is an important part of us. It plays a significant role in keeping us in the okay situation: safe and happy. However, as Maria's story also shows, our Roommate can cause problems even while it tries to protect us. It can cause us to dwell on the negative, to repeatedly blame others, and to pretend to be someone other than who we really are. These reactions often hurt ourselves and others. The next chapter explains why.

EXERCISE: TALK CHECK

Throughout this book, I will provide exercises to help you through the process of considering and then managing your inner voice. The exercises serve as reminders or tools to guide you as you practice these new skills.

At Level 1, the goal is to observe the conversation. At first, you might see it hours or days later, but ultimately you want to notice it on time, as it's happening.

To complete the Talk Check, start by asking yourself, *Is it there?* If you find the conversation, then write it down word for word—including your attempts to stop it. To capture your inner chats, you can carry a notebook or create a digital file on your computer or smartphone. You may think, *Oh, this is going to take so much time!* Yes, it will take time, but it is worth the effort—much more than you might suppose. This Talk Check is the key to improving your relationships. You can't manage the self-talk and the resulting behaviors if you don't trace what's happening.

If you don't realize that the conversation happened until days later, that's okay. As soon as you realize there was a dialogue, write down what you remember. The important thing is to get in the habit of writing it down.

Reminder: all of the exercises in this and the following chapters are gathered at the back of the book in Appendix A.

Chapter 2

IT REALLY IS A CRAB!

ON A LOVELY WINTER NIGHT, MY COLLEAGUES AND I met at a restaurant for dinner. At one side of the large round table, people discussed current issues in Germany, Europe, and around the world. Some blamed the governments, claiming their decisions have gone from bad to terrible. Others blamed people in general, claiming they have lost hope in their countries, the environment, and the planet. Without hope, they lack motivation to support this or that country or help their world.

"Conditions were so much better in our grandparents' era," a colleague named Felix said. "People strongly believed in God back then."

Ben laughed. "So, we should pray every day to reach better conditions?" he asked. That's the solution, right?"

"Well, it is one of the major pillars and could be the foundation," Felix replied.

"The foundation that has killed many people and damaged our world much more than anything else in history, huh?"

The argument continued for several minutes, with Ben and

Felix talking over each other and gesticulating wildly. Finally, Felix stood up. "That's it! I don't have to listen to this."

"No, no, Felix," someone else said. "Sit down, please!" And then a few colleagues jumped in and changed the subject so we could enjoy the rest of our evening.

Over the next several months, Felix and I went out together for drinks with other friends. Every time, Felix somehow brought Ben into the conversation and talked about him in a negative way. He tried to do it in a joking manner, but he clearly held a grudge against Ben and wanted to make him look bad. Felix did this so often that other friends started gossiping about Ben too. Even after Ben apologized, Felix would not let it go, thinking it was not a genuine apology.

What caused Felix to react this way? The conversation going on inside his head. It started immediately after that dinner and continued for at least six months because Felix did not observe it. As a result, he negatively impacted several relationships, his reputation, and his mental health, as you will see.

IMPORTANCE OF THE CONVERSATION

In Chapter 1, we made an important discovery: there is a conversation going on inside our head. In most situations, we play the role of listener in this conversation, and our Roommate—our inner voice—plays the role of speaker.

Now it's time to understand why this conversation is so important.

RELATIONSHIPS, REPUTATIONS, MENTAL HEALTH

After the dinner incident occurred, Felix felt justified in punishing Ben for insulting him and his religion. Ben knew how important religion was to Felix and still made those comments, so he deserved blame, right? Plus, Felix felt like he needed to protect himself and what was important to him. To confirm his feelings, Felix asked other people if he was right in punishing Ben. Most agreed, so Felix felt further justified.

As a result, he severely damaged a long-time friendship—all because he let the inner conversation go unchecked.

In addition, Felix ruined Ben's reputation, as well as his own. Felix told many people what Ben had said about Felix's beliefs. He even added some of his own assumptions related to Ben's attitudes toward work meetings and the company as a whole. Sharing these ideas with others caused them to look at Ben differently. At the same time, however, people started viewing Felix differently. He listened to the Roommate and reacted. He started behaving in a way that contradicted the rules he believed as part of his religion. People no longer trusted Felix as they did before. They saw how he talked behind his friend's back and wondered if he would do the same to them.

Felix was an educated, disciplined person. He was also known as being very kind. Yet here he was blaming Ben and talking negatively about him. Felix became confused by his own behavior. The conversation in his head told him he was right to be upset. After all, this guy had insulted his religion. But listening to his Roommate also caused him to act in ways that contradicted that same religion. Because Felix let this conversation go on for so long, his confusion grew, and his mental health suffered as a result. He added unnecessary and unrelated layers about Ben's work behavior, which increased the mental chatter. He became distracted during everyday activities and started having problems concentrating at work.

When I told Felix that his inner conversations about the dinner dispute were causing the problems in his friendships, reputation, and mental health, he didn't believe me. He was sure it was Ben's fault. But he grew tired of his mental suffering and wanted to be done with this long-lasting challenge, so he agreed to write down what he remembered about the conversations inside his head and with others.

When he looked inside, Felix found that some version of the following dialogue took place throughout the day, every day:

> **Roommate:** He knows you are religious. He is probably jealous of you and your position in the company. He is highly educated but still does not comprehend respecting others.
>
> **Felix:** Oh no, he has been so kind in many cases.
>
> **Roommate:** Nope! You're wrong about that. He insulted what is so precious to you. He knows that and did it purposefully to destroy your position.
>
> **Felix:** Ah, please stop it. It just happened and it's done. Does not matter any longer.
>
> **Roommate:** If you don't do something, he will do that again, and soon, others will dare to do that to you too.
>
> **Felix:** I can't fight against everybody for their insults.
>
> **Roommate:** Heh, do you really believe in your beliefs or not? If not, okay, let's stay silent.

When he reviewed a series of written conversations, Felix was shocked at the toxic and negative dialogue he found.

Then Felix considered his conversations with others, specifically, how many times he talked behind his friend's back in a month. He counted more than twenty instances—almost once a day. This was a breaking point for Felix. He began to see that his actions were far more destructive than Ben's comments in that one conversation. And he began to see that the inner conversation he harbored was causing him to act in self-destructive ways.

One reason Felix didn't initially believe this conversation was causing problems is that he thought the speaker was himself. He felt like he was protecting himself and his religion. He had been insulted, so his response—the inner conversation—was valid. This sometimes happens when the dialogue revolves around a sensitive topic. The self-talk in such cases starts quickly and powerfully, and it often lasts longer when we receive confirmation from others or find proof that we are right. In such cases, we often feel outraged at being insulted, and justified in our reaction. Deep down we may also feel sadness, but anger is easier to feel than sadness. Rage pushes the inner conversation forward, and it becomes stronger without us realizing it. We may have graduated from a top university and may hold a high-level position, and we still might not see how this conversation affects our life.

If we don't notice that the conversation has started, we won't be able to respond differently next time. We will develop a habit of reacting and putting up our guard, and that guard will become stronger each time a similar conversation or situation occurs. We will remember what happened the last time those fears arose, and we will be quicker to defend ourselves. We will continue to say things we regret, push people away, and act in ways that go against our values. We will continue to suffer mentally, which can cause us to be distracted, unfocused, and scattered, leading to mistakes and bad decisions. If we don't observe and analyze this conversation, it will continue to negatively impact every area of our lives, day after day, year after year.

The next time someone talks to Felix about his religion, for example, he might remember Ben's insult. His walls might go up immediately because he trained his Roommate to react, to be on guard, where his religion is concerned. His Roommate might even create new mind games using various input feeds, adding to the conversation, making up stories about the person or situation that aren't even true. As a result, Felix might completely miss the person's point because of the chatter running through his head. Soon, he might avoid all conversations about religion even though it is one of the most important aspects of his life.

Here's the good news: if we learn to consider the conversation and realize it's happening—even if we cannot yet manage it—we have the option of responding differently. We have a chance to change the output and not be a crab.

MISSED OPPORTUNITIES

In addition to ruining our reputation, relationships, and mental health, not observing this conversation can cause us to miss opportunities. In response to certain inputs, our Roommate might lead us to prejudge a person or situation and then make a poor decision or do something that adversely affects a possibility before us.

This happened to me several years ago when I had a fantastic job opportunity. A friend introduced me to an IT group full of high-level businesspeople who wanted to hire a business lead to work closely with their Chief Technical Officer (CTO). It was a critical position that had widespread influence.

"Hooman is completely trustworthy for this position," my friend told them. "He's perfect for the job."

When I met with this group, they asked several questions related to my lifestyle and relationships. They wanted to see if I was as trustworthy as my friend said, nothing more. However, as soon as they started asking questions that seemed irrelevant to me at the time, my Roommate appeared and suggested alternate reasons for their inquiries: They doubted I could do the job because I was young. They didn't think I had enough experience. They were being nosy and pulling out private details that were none of their business.

After the meeting, my inner conversation spiraled out of control. I became convinced that those businesspeople intended to extract my private info and ideas, and maybe even misuse my time, energy, and money. Instead of considering the facts—that they were simply trying to verify that I could be trusted—I made up stories and then became stressed and anxious. Two days later, in my confused state, I emailed these leaders a long list of questions and asked them to answer every single one in detail.

As you might guess, they never responded.

A while later, one of the representatives told me about the exchange from their perspective. They had enjoyed a warm, professional face-to-face meeting with me, and then received my email full of questions. They found it surprising that I would expect these highly experienced professionals to answer each one. What a mistake! Later on, I also learned that the young business lead who ultimately took the position became a millionaire.

In this situation, my Roommate was supposedly protecting me from threats, but this protection should have come in the form of facts, reports, and statistics. Instead, feelings, judgments, and mind games drove my inner conversation. Based on these speculations, I guessed wrongly at my position with these businessmen. Such a significant financial opportunity only comes around once a decade, and I mishandled it because of my unchecked inner conversation.

Missed opportunities also happen in relationships. We can mess up chances for friendships, romantic partnerships, and long-term collaborations because we listen to our Roommate and prejudge or make poor decisions based on faulty inputs. We follow our emotions and focus on what makes us feel comfortable, not facts.

My friend Colin found this out the hard way. He felt safe in his single life and commitment-free relationship with his girlfriend. When she brought up marriage, he felt threatened, and his Roommate fed him faulty ideas to protect him: He was better off single. He was smart enough to keep his girlfriend and enjoy his freedom. He didn't need to get married to be happy. Marriage would only bring a burden.

Based on this advice, Colin played around and assumed his girlfriend loved him enough to wait. Even when a series of disputes sabotaged his relationship, Colin still didn't look at the facts. Finally, his girlfriend broke up with him. His Roommate said she would be back, but that never happened. Colin lost his true love when she married someone else, which significantly damaged his mental health.

What is the underlying reason for missing opportunities like Colin did? We don't want to leave our comfort zone. In that safe space, we feel a high level of satisfaction and happiness. Like people addicted to drugs or alcohol, we only care about maintaining that feeling right now, even though the source of that happiness could actually be causing harm.

To break this cycle, we must learn to consider our self-talk. We must recognize the unhealthy inputs coming from our inner voice and replace them with valid information. Yes, making this shift will push us out of our comfort zone, but our relationships, careers, and general well-being will all benefit in the long run.

THE CONFUSION THAT RESULTS

Before Ben made a negative comment about his friend's religion, Felix was okay. His relationship with Ben was fine. They were close friends, and Felix had no reason to believe his friend would do such a bad thing to him. When Ben delivered that insult, suddenly, Felix was not okay.

Felix's actions and reactions after that were all part of his unconscious attempt to get back to his comfort zone. He listened to his Roommate, but the situation got worse instead of better.

If Felix had noticed when the inner conversation started, he could have avoided the confusion that caused many problems. Because he didn't, he damaged his relationship with Ben and his reputation with friends who had previously seen him as kind and wise.

If we don't learn to see this conversation happening, we will do the same. Confusion will cause us to act in the same harmful ways. Our guard will come up more quickly. We will continue to hurt those we love. And we won't understand why.

However, if we do start to notice when the conversation happens, we can start to manage it. We share that solution in Chapter 3.

EXERCISES

At Level 2, the goal is to observe how our inner self-talk impacts our lives. The exercises remind us to check whether a dialogue is happening and how it might be causing suffering for us and/or others.

At this level, we don't worry about stopping the conversation or changing its direction. Trying to stop or change it can distract us from noticing what is going on in the conversation itself. For now, we focus on observing the inner dialogue and analyzing how it is affecting our lives.

Talk Check

Continue using the Talk Check. Any time you notice a conversation is happening, write it down as soon as possible. If you want to progress in noticing and managing this inner voice so that it doesn't cause problems, you have to see the conversations in writing.

Thumb in Fist

When you find yourself in a situation that makes you uncomfortable, make a fist and slip your thumb inside. This is a reminder to be aware that your Roommate might start talking.

You can also use Thumb in Fist to do a Talk Check when you aren't in a position to write down the conversation—for example, if you're driving or in the middle of a meeting. Consider the conversation in the moment and then write it down when you have a chance.

Remember: don't worry about stopping or changing the direction of the conversation. Use this exercise as a reminder to observe your inner dialogue and see how it is impacting your life.

Three-Seconds Rule

To train yourself to be present and aware, wait three seconds before you start any new action—for example, before you start the car, brush your teeth, share your opinions, or react to a news story.

This pause can help you become a skilled observer of yourself and your inner self-talk. As you practice this exercise, you will start noticing the conversation more often and the ways you react in response. The three-second pause also gives you time to think of a better action or response if there is one.

Chapter 3

HELP! GET ME OUT OF THIS BUCKET!

WHEN SARAH WAS ABOUT NINE YEARS OLD, SHE started questioning the way her father treated her. She felt he was strict and unfair. He always said no when she wanted to go to a friend's birthday party or play outside or even play with a friend in her bedroom behind a closed door.

As a teenager, Sarah made a more deliberate effort to escape her father's watchful eye. She even lied about having homework and said she needed to close her bedroom door to concentrate. She also lied to boys who asked her out and to friends who asked why she didn't attend so-and-so's party. She couldn't tell any of them the truth: that her dad wouldn't let her go.

Before high school, Sarah thought it was normal for fathers not to support their daughters in their interests. Through conversations with her friends, she learned the truth. Other fathers did encourage their daughters to play sports or join the dance team or participate in school government. Her friends' dads helped them buy supplies for their hobbies. Sarah felt sick when she learned what she was missing.

After she turned eighteen and started university, Sarah tried to stand up to her father. "Now I have the right to decide for myself," she told him. "You cannot tell me what to do anymore."

"Under my roof, you live by my rules," he replied.

She wanted to move out but didn't have enough money, so she felt stuck, living with the one serious enemy she had in the world: her father.

By the time I met Sarah, she was twenty-seven years old, and she truly hated her dad. Her inner conversation about how he treated her had gone on for nearly twenty years. She had trained her Roommate to react a certain way, and she now put up her guard before any interaction with him even started.

Over the years, Sarah also added to the conversation. She told herself that her father didn't trust her and that he only cared about his own reputation, not Sarah's well-being. When she was younger, he had created rules about what she could and couldn't wear and what she could or couldn't say, especially when they were with relatives and family friends. At the time, he said he didn't want people taking advantage of her, but now Sarah's inner voice said he was only trying to protect his status in the eyes of others.

Because Sarah didn't consider this conversation about her dad, its influence spread. She started believing that all men around her father's age were also controlling and cheerless, so she avoided them. Even when she met gentlemen who were kind and supportive, she felt uncomfortable and didn't trust them. She decided it was better to keep her distance from all men because they might become controlling like her father.

In her book *Dare to Lead,* Brené Brown suggests that daring leaders work from the assumption that people are doing the best they can. I shared this thought with Sarah and suggested that maybe her father was doing the best he could, even though it didn't seem that way.

All of a sudden, something clicked for Sarah. On at least two occasions when she was younger, Sarah thought she heard her father crying through his closed bedroom door. She asked her mother if this was true. "Your father has some problems," she replied. "I cannot do anything between you guys. You need to go to therapy."

Over a series of conversations with her mom, Sarah learned more about her father's childhood. When he was a teenager, a high school girl from his small town was gang-raped on her way to school. Afterward, she struggled with severe psychological problems that persisted until Sarah's father left the area.

After the incident, Sarah's father overheard his parents talking about it. His takeaway was that if the girl's parents had been more protective—for example, if they had forbidden her from taking the shortcut through the jungle on the way to school—she wouldn't have been raped. At this point, a conversation started in his head that he nurtured for decades. It then affected his relationship with his daughter, causing him to become overly protective.

On one level, Sarah realized her father was doing the best he could, but her inner voice still prevented her from seeing his positive qualities. She saw everything through one filter: his desire to control.

After six months of meeting and doing exercises, Sarah learned to separate the speaker and the listener in the conversation going on inside her head. She became proficient in identifying when her Roommate started speaking, in using the exercises, and in preventing that conversation from causing problems in her relationship with her father and others. She learned to lower her guard with her dad, which enabled her to understand that all those years, he had been trying to protect her. She was able to accept him as he is.

Sarah's father didn't change. He still made the same kinds of comments that came across as controlling. But because she was in CCC training, Sarah didn't react. She had learned to see her Roommate as separate from herself and had started distinguishing between the voices in her head.

Her father noticed the change and asked what happened. He expected them to fight as they always had. Sarah explained the training she had gone through and how she had learned to observe and monitor the conversation in her head. As a result of this interaction, space opened for better dialogue between father and daughter. In one case, Sarah's dad actually started weeping in front of her, which he would not have done before. She was able to give him a hug and comfort him, which had never happened.

This whole scenario between Sarah and her dad could have been avoided if one or both of them had learned to observe their inner voice (Level 1) and then analyze the problems it was causing (Level 2). Because they didn't, they killed the space between them. Their conversations together were strained, and their whole relationship suffered for two decades. Once Sarah started training, she stopped reacting, and the relationship improved.

In this chapter, we'll explore Level 3 of the CCC training: the importance of considering our inner conversation in the moment so that we can learn to distinguish between ourselves and our Roommate. In doing this, we will start converting confusion into clarity and improve the quality of our relationships.

FIND, CONSIDER, DISTINGUISH

From the examples of Felix (Chapter 2) and Sarah, it is clear that this inner conversation is always ready to run. To keep this dialogue from negatively impacting our lives, we must find it on time. It's not enough to notice the conversation ten days or even ten minutes after it has happened. By then, the damage has likely been done. We've probably made hurtful comments or caused ourselves mental suffering. We need to observe the conversation as it's happening.

As mentioned earlier, we usually take the role of the listener, and our Roommate is the speaker. Here we get more specific: to manage the conversation inside our head, we need to embrace the role of listener. We need to consciously listen to what's going on inside our head. Only when we do this in real time can we start to distinguish between ourselves and our Roommate, and distinguishing is the key to stopping our crabby behavior. When we are able to make a distinction, we see which voice should be heeded and which should be ignored.

The more people involved in a discussion, the more difficult it is to distinguish between the voices. For example, if we're in a meeting and one of our coworkers makes a comment, our Roommate begins speaking. When the next person talks, our inner dialogue shifts. Without us making a conscious decision, our Roommate adds new points to the conversation. It accesses memories, past events, and previous discussions stored in our brain, and brings them to mind as a way to respond to the current situation.

To avoid confusion and to enjoy healthy outputs, we must take the role of listener and consider each voice. Is that suggestion coming from the speaker, our Roommate? Or is it coming from our own mind? If we don't listen, we might react to one of the Roommate's points in unhelpful or destructive ways.

In addition, if we don't take the role of listener and learn to distinguish, we get stuck in the same responses and reactions. We hold on to the same grudges and old wounds. We put up the same guard. We have no space to follow Brené Brown's advice and accept that someone is doing the best they can.

When we fail to distinguish, we allow negative, confusing thoughts to crowd our mind. We become preoccupied with protecting ourselves when we don't really need protection. As a result, we don't have space for joy, peace, and empathy. We don't have room to consider the possibilities and solutions all around us. We block the positive flow of energy in the form of our talents and capabilities. We prevent ourselves from advancing in our careers, helping others, and progressing into greater depths in our relationships.

However, if we learn to distinguish our Roommate's voice from our own, we can bring healing to our friendships and partnerships. We can keep ourselves from reacting to other people's reactions—just as Sarah did with her father. We can start building or rebuilding strong, joyful relationships. We can be awake to the daily graces and gifts that come our way.

One point to remember: When people insult us or blame us, they are trying to find release. Maybe they had a bad day. Possibly they are trying to get back to their own comfort zone. Even if we have done something that led to the other person's words or actions, their reaction is still not about us. They're trying to help themselves. If we learn to pause and differentiate between the voices, we can keep ourselves from reacting. Our Roommate may speak up and suggest that we defend ourselves or respond unkindly. If we distinguish this voice from our own, we can ignore it. We can let the person's comment go without a reaction or apologize more quickly when we see our fault.

A trainee named Sandra was insulted by a family member

named Antonio. Afterward, her Roommate reminded her of everything negative and destructive that Antonio had done in the past. She forgot all of his positive attributes. Sandra could not distinguish between her own thoughts and the suggestions coming from her Roommate. She felt stuck and didn't know what to do.

After I talked with her, Sandra agreed to write down her inner conversation. When she read the dialogue and took the position of listener, she was finally able to distinguish between the voices. Even then, she found that almost none of the advice offered was acceptable.

Before engaging in training, Sandra nurtured a plan to get revenge on Antonio. Afterward, she invited him to coffee and shared how Antonio's insult had affected her. Antonio responded well, and Sandra's revenge plan was replaced by peace. In addition, Sandra felt confident that if Antonio, or anyone else, insulted her in the future, she would be able to differentiate between the voices. She would understand which unhelpful suggestions were coming from her Roommate and ignore them.

LET THE HEALING BEGIN

When people are heartbroken, they can find it particularly challenging to distinguish the voices in their heads. Based on my experience and the observations of therapists and psychologists, mental suffering around the death of a child is exceedingly complex. One of my trainees lost her son in an accident, and her inner voice convinced her that life had ended. "I only keep on living because my husband and a few others need me," Petra told me. "Otherwise, I would leave my life right now."

Petra wrote down the self-talk inside her head. In a series of sessions, we identified the unreasonable suggestions that came from her Roommate: "You should ask your husband to leave you as you are sick and no longer normal." "If you had resisted the idea of birthing a child, this nightmare would not have happened."

As she continued using the Talk Check, she learned to separate the recommendations of her intentional thoughts from those arbitrarily suggested by her Roommate. As she learned to take different Perspectives on the situation (more on Perspectives in the Chapter 4 exercises), Petra also learned to distinguish between the voices in the moment, not just when she wrote them down afterward. Rejecting the negative suggestions freed up mental space for enjoying memories of her son. She recently shared, "With all my heart, I want to meet him again. Whether it is possible or not, I intend to live on the high road and feel him deeply in the inner space I have reserved for him. I have also created room for other precious experiences, like helping my husband, who suffers a lot too, and other parents in the same situation."

At Level 3, our main goal is not only to notice the conversation on time, but to separate our voice from the voice of our Roommate. As we do so, we can start changing how we respond in the present. We can also begin healing wounds, like the death of a child, as well as past grudges and hurts. Sometimes the healing is immediate. Sometimes it takes days, weeks, or months. But if we practice Talk Check, Three-Seconds Rule, Thumb in Fist, and the other exercises presented in this book, change will come.

You will probably find that you catch the conversation on time in certain relationships or situations but miss it in others. That's normal. Don't be discouraged! Just keep practicing, and soon you'll find healing in all areas.

Now that you are able to distinguish, I'll show you how to manage this conversation and begin training your inner voice to consistently respond without blaming, judging, or other crabby behaviors.

EXERCISES

The following exercises will help you remember to consider the inner conversation moment by moment. Perhaps more importantly, they will help you distinguish between your voice and your Roommate's.

Continue using the Talk Check. This exercise is essential at every level. Three-Seconds Rule and Thumb in Fist were also included in Chapter 2, but here the focus is using these tools to help you listen and differentiate between the voices.

Thumb in Fist
As stated, the Thumb in Fist exercise is very helpful in learning to become aware moment by moment. When you are in conversation with others, for example, or listening to a speaker at a seminar, place your thumb in your fist to subtly check whether you are also conversing with your Roommate. When you are alone, use this exercise to check whether you are replaying an old conversation. Even when you are alone and relaxed, mind empty, the conversation can suddenly begin. Your Roommate is always ready to find something to talk about, all in the name of protecting you.

Here's one example of how I used Thumb in Fist to help me observe my inner chat, listen to the voices, and change my response in the moment: Several years ago, I came upon a group of guys shouting at each other. As I walked closer, I realized that one of the men was yelling racist comments at the others. When he noticed me, he pointed and said, "And that f**king guy too!"

My Roommate immediately started a dialogue, and I became agitated:

> **Roommate:** He just insulted you! You hold a high-level Kung Fu degree. You can fight him off.
>
> **Me:** But I will not initiate a fight. I only use my skills to defend myself if someone attacks me first.
>
> **Roommate:** You have many witnesses here. Look at this crowd! If you injure him badly, they will know that you only acted out of self-defense.

At this point, I put my thumb in my fist. I traced the conversation and realized my Roommate was trying to protect me. My Roommate was suggesting that I fight back. The guy started walking toward me. I knew the potentially terrible results if I listened to my inner voice and gave myself permission to fight. So, I quickly left the scene.

Less than thirty seconds later, the man hurling insults stabbed one of the other men. If I had listened to my Roommate, that situation could have ended badly for me.

Three-Seconds Rule
In most situations, your brain immediately supplies an answer or a reaction—something to say or do in response to what's happening. By pausing for three seconds, you train yourself to wait, not to react immediately. This allows you to consider whether that other voice

is really your own. It also gives you time to evaluate what's going on: What's on your mind? What conversation is running there? What are you telling yourself about the situation? Pausing also gives you time to use some of the other exercises to better manage the conversation that has started.

Mohammad, one of the CCC trainees, practiced the Three-Seconds Rule daily, and in one case, it prevented a terrible accident. He sat in his SUV in the parking lot, working on his laptop and listening to loud music. When he finished, his inner voice immediately spoke up. "You should get back to the office immediately and share the results of your fantastic work before any of your colleagues do!" Even though Mohammad was excited and wanted to get back quickly, he paused. He listened to the voices and distinguished his Roommate's from his own. In that three-second pause, he also remembered that children often play in this parking lot.

Mohammad stopped the music, got out of his car, walked around to the back, and found two small children rolling around on the ground and laughing.

Here's another example: I once spotted a child struggling in a pool. My first instinct was to climb the fence to go help him, but it would have taken me a few minutes. Instead, I paused. Then I realized if I shouted, someone closer to the pool might hear me and go help him. That's exactly what happened. In response to my shouts, the boy was saved in about thirty seconds. If it had taken three minutes, he might not have been saved at all.

Mirroring
As mentioned earlier, we receive inputs from various sources—memories, conversations, social media, and so on. Sometimes we

get stuck in one of these inputs: our own thoughts or perspectives. The Mirroring exercise reminds us to get out of our own heads and observe ourselves from the outside, as any other person would see us. This is the basic exercise for Perspective 1 (which you'll learn more about in Chapter 4) and is one we can do every day several times a day to see ourselves from the outside.

In the exercise, imagine watching yourself as you participate in routine activities: driving, talking to a coworker, and typing at your desk. When you take this outside perspective, you can watch yourself talking and interacting with others. You can see your facial expressions. You gain a 360-degree perspective of yourself, rather than being confined to what's going on inside your head.

Viewing yourself from the outside helps you check your responses and reactions, as well as the inner conversation that is causing them. With this awareness, you are better able to take the next step, managing your self-talk and reactions, which we'll discuss in Chapter 4.

Mirroring also provides an opportunity to observe the way you are talking to yourself. You probably look at yourself in the mirror several times a day. When you do, ask yourself, "Am I insulting myself right now? Am I telling myself stories?" If you have time at the moment, write down what you find. If not, make a mental note to do so later.

Fixed Short Phrases
In Chapter 4, I will introduce several Not to Dos—actions and reactions we take in our efforts to protect ourselves and return to the okay situation. Based on these Not to Dos and aspects of the training we have already discussed, you can create fixed short phrases

to repeat to yourself when the inner conversation has begun, and you are confused. These phrases can help you stop the self-talk before you say or do something that will hurt yourself or others.

For example, one of the CCC trainees repeats the phrase "No negative" whenever he finds himself engaged in negative self-talk or actions such as blaming and judging others. Another trainee says, "Calm down! I am listening to you!" to prevent his inner voice from flaring up when it is not required for protection.

One of my favorite fixed short phrases is "Hey! Nothing ultimately will belong to me except the impossible graces and blessings I am receiving now." I use this phrase to remind my Roommate that I do not need its suggestions on how to protect my position, reputation, wealth, and material possessions because none of those things will belong to me in the end. I do not need to make myself look good. Instead, I can keep myself aware of the gifts and blessings all around me.

Another favorite is "Bang! Bang!" It comes from the name of a control system that mechanically or electronically turns something on or off when a certain target has been reached. For me, "Bang! Bang!" is a way to remind my inner voice that I am in control, and I don't have to react to its suggestions.

I have a list of fixed short phrases that I meditate on each morning and then repeat throughout the day. As you move through the training, you will come up with phrases that are more beneficial to you.

Chapter 4

OMG! I FOUND A WAY OUT!

"WHEN YOU SET A TIMELINE AND WE PUSH BACK because we know it's unattainable, you get so insistent that we stop pushing. It's not working. You have a lot of strengths, but you're not good at estimating time, and we need to find a new process that works for all of us."[5]

This was the honest feedback Brené Brown received from her CFO at a meeting with the whole team. In her book *Dare to Lead*, Brown shares that hearing these words was uncomfortable, but she appreciated the CFO's clarity. Why? Because being clear is kind.

According to Brown, most of us avoid this kind of honesty and clarity because we think we're being kind. The truth is, when we're unclear, we're actually being unkind. The reason we share unclear half-truths, blame someone for not meeting

---

5 Brené Brown, *Dare to Lead: Brave Work. Tough Conversations. Whole Hearts.* (New York: Random House, 2018), 45–46.

an expectation we never explained, or talk *about* someone and not *to* them is that these actions make *us* feel more comfortable. These actions may protect *us* temporarily, but they don't actually help the other person.

What causes us to be unclear? The inner conversation started by our Roommate. If we cannot distinguish between the speakers, then we become confused and react to the self-talk inside our head. We speak in the way that makes us most comfortable. Sometimes by sharing part of a truth, we receive credit or praise, while sharing the other pieces poses a threat to our well-being—at least in our mind. So, our well-trained Roommate leads us to share only the beneficial parts and keep silent about the rest.

Sometimes we may feel like we're being kind—and maybe we are in that specific instance. But five minutes or five days later, when the inner conversation starts up again, we're plunged back into confusion. We shift back to being unkind, even though we don't understand why or how.

No matter how hard we try, we cannot be clear and therefore kind when we are confused. In response to the input feeds it receives, our brain starts analyzing and processing. It doesn't care about the health or accuracy of the feeds. It simply analyzes and processes in the way that comes naturally. Confusion results and our outputs are consequently unclear.

What is the solution? Brown says the answer is to be straightforward and honest, but we can't do that if we don't deal with the confusion that drives us to be unclear and unkind in the first place. When we're confused, we are prone to judging and prejudging others, protecting ourselves by saying what is less likely to get a reaction, and so on. These actions are not kind.

By reading books like *Dare to Lead* or listening to speakers like Tony Robbins, we might be able to change our behaviors for a day or a week. But because the inner conversation is still there—because our brain still functions with the same mechanism to protect—this change will not last. We still have faulty processing, and our mind still plays tricks. We continue putting up our guard and acting in ways that confuse us. According to neuroscientist Antonio Damasio, this is because we don't deal with the root: "We are not thinking machines. We are feeling machines that think. Most leaders accept it but forget it." So, we don't know how unattended feelings and fears cause major problems. As a result, we will keep repeating unwanted behaviors without knowing why.

To experience actual change, to become clear instead of unclear and kind instead of unkind, we have to deal with the root.

As mentioned, we cannot eliminate the Roommate, but we can manage it. We can decrease the frequency with which it causes us to be unclear and unkind. In doing so, we can actually transform our personality and character. We can behave and talk differently than we always have. You've already seen this in Sarah's relationship with her father: she learned to stop reacting when he said something controlling. She learned to let it go and instead focus on fixing the faulty processing of old data in her own mind.

This transformation didn't happen overnight. Sarah diligently practiced certain techniques to manage her reactions. In this chapter, I'll show you how to do the same. Through the methods presented here, you can convert confusion into clarity and change your responses in the moment.

NOT TO DOS

When we feel threatened, stressed, or confused, we all resort to certain actions and reactions to protect ourselves. The first step to managing our Roommate is noticing when we do or say these things. We need to recognize the external results of the internal conversation. Do we blame others or ourselves? Do we judge others? Do we keep ruminating on what happened?

Once we see these reactions, we can train ourselves to stop doing them—or at least put bigger gaps in how often we do them. We can disrupt the habits formed over the years and become new and improved versions of ourselves.

What happens if we don't use these techniques? We remain stuck and continue experiencing the negative impacts of our reactions. We strengthen our guard and repeat the same actions over and over without understanding why. Our relationships and our own mental health suffer greatly.

Based on my own inner conversations and those written by others, I have compiled a list of 10+1 Not to Dos—actions we should stop doing if we desire stronger, happier, and more peaceful relationships.[6] In this section, I present the foundational Not to Do, as well as two others that people do most commonly. The whole list of 10+1 Not to Dos can be found in Appendix B.

0. DON'T ACT/REACT

When you find yourself confused, unsettled, or feeling threatened, stop. Don't act or react. This is a great chance to use the Three-Seconds Rule. Just pause and recognize the situation for

---

[6] Our lists begin with zero on purpose. It is the +1 in 10+1. Think of zero as the step before you do anything else; it is the strong foundation from which you will launch.

what it is. Be aware that if you act/react, your response might be full of mistakes and judgments. To avoid being a crab who pulls down others with your words, it's best to stop. Say nothing. Do nothing. In most cases, you have time to think of a beneficial solution. You don't have to feel pressured. If anybody pushes you to act and immediate action is not necessary, ask them to stop, and share that you will act later if needed.

I was recently pulled over for running a red light. When the police officer asked me why I ran the red light, I didn't rush to give him an answer. Instead, I told him, "I'm thinking about why." This was the truth. I had never run a red light before and was trying to figure out why I had this time.

After a minute or so, I looked up at the policeman and said, "I found why! I was talking to myself. I was focused on my inner conversation instead of my driving."

I'm sure the police officer had never heard such a response after stopping a driver. To be released from the situation as soon as possible, we often have immediate, ready-made responses, or we quickly accept the fine. Sometimes we even apologize, even though we have done nothing wrong to the police officer. This is simply our conditioned reaction, based on the inputs stored in the brain's many layers. When faced with a similar situation, we respond the same as we always have. Instead, we should stop. With this pause, we can accept that we are confused and then wait until we find the best way to respond.

In some situations, you may think you have a social responsibility to act immediately. Even then, however, remind yourself to pause. A quick reaction to soothe your anger is not the answer, and it can often worsen the situation. I once found a guy releasing himself by scratching cars in the alley. I used the Three-Seconds Rule, which gave me time to come to several conclusions: *The guy is upset and is releasing himself. I shouldn't try to stop him. He has a knife. Most of these cars are probably insured.* I also came up with a plan: I asked him to stop and then called the police when he continued. My car wasn't parked in the alley, but I would have responded the same way if it had been.

This Not to Do mostly applies to our communications, relationships, and social interactions—not true emergencies when quick action is needed. That said, even in some emergency situations, it is better to do nothing if we feel confused. Think of earthquakes and car accidents when we may not know the extent of someone's injuries. Bystanders sometimes do more damage by moving the victims rather than waiting for paramedics trained to handle these cases.

After we have worked on converting confusion into clarity and can consistently recognize an actual threat, we may be in a position to act or react immediately. This happened in one of my training sessions. Someone made a racist comment, and without hesitation, I asked him to stop and apologize. I was clear that such a statement could not be allowed. I needed to protect and defend others in the room, as well as humanity at large. Note that I didn't respond out of anger, as any rage springs from confusion, and in this situation, I was quite clear about the threat. Reacting out of anger would have led to unhelpful comments.

In most life situations, when we feel confused, we don't actually need to act or react, even though we feel like we must do something. Whether in a conversation with another person or listening to a news story that is causing concern, we don't need to react.

One note: When you start practicing this pause, you might find that people react negatively. Your inaction might bother them. They might try to convince you that you need to do something. That's okay. They have to deal with their own internal conversation.

1. DON'T BLAME

Based on the Talk Checks I've seen over the years, blaming is our most common reaction when we get pushed out of the okay place. We lash out in an attempt to release ourselves from discomfort.

Many years ago, author Werner Erhard said, "What most people do is give space to people's quality and deal with their garbage. Actually, you should do it the other way around. Deal with who they are and give space to their garbage. Keep interacting with them as if they were perfect." When we blame, we are doing the former: we are dealing with their garbage. Instead, we should give space. When we feel threatened, we feel the need to protect, and our natural reaction is to lash out and blame—not find positive qualities and treat people as if they were perfect. If we give space, we will be less likely to blame in response to our inner conversation.

One couple, Sam and Bahaar, took the CCC training course together, though Sam seemed more diligent about doing the homework and exercises. During my conversations with Bahaar, I learned that she held a grudge against her partner. Sam was at Level 4, but based on his actions at home, Bahaar thought he should be at Level 1.

From reading her Talk Checks, I learned more about her inner chats. She had been blaming her partner for years about many aspects of their relationship. Bahaar could have written a book full of all the ways she blamed Sam—and herself.

In addition, she disclosed that she believed she could have had a much better partner. Even though she loved Sam, she made him out to be the bad guy in many situations. This thought poisoned every area of their relationship.

Through the training, I learned that many problems in their relationship stemmed from a certain mindset Bahaar had developed earlier in her dating life. She had gotten into the habit of blaming men for everything: not being a gentleman, not being brave, not proposing, and so on. This started when she was a teenager. She compared immature adolescent boys to her father, who was a kind gentleman.

The importance is not when or why this habit formed but the fact that it had continued for a long time. This inner conversation in which Bahaar blamed guys for not reaching some unstated standard had become her default response. She had carried it into her current relationship. When Sam finally became angry and told her to stop blaming him, Bahaar responded with more criticism—this time, for telling her to stop when he didn't see his own faults.

Despite this evident pattern, Bahaar still fought the idea that her blaming was causing problems in her relationships. She thought it was *their* behavior—her boyfriends over the years, and now Sam. Finally, she became so miserable that she didn't care what was going on. She simply wanted to stop the conversation and the mental anguish it caused.

Bahaar accepted my invitation to trace her inner self-talk. She asked herself several questions and wrote down her answers: *Is Sam the only cause of the suffering inside your head? Do you only converse with yourself about him in this annoying way? Even though you respect your father, do any of his mistakes bother you?*

In considering these questions, Bahaar began to notice the habits that had formed in her relationships with men: judging, blaming, criticizing, and so on. She also realized that she had taken the role of victim in life and particularly in her partnership with Sam: she assumed things like "I deserve to be treated more nicely." "Bad things always happen to me." "I'm really the victim here!"

To show Bahaar how her inner conversation about being a victim was impacting her life, I told her about a psychology experiment from the 1980s.[7] In this study, researchers put realistic-looking scars on the participants' faces. They told the subjects they wanted to discover how strangers reacted to them with these scars. Just before the participants went out in public, the researchers acted as if they were touching up the scars to make them look more realistic. Instead, they actually removed all the scars.

When the participants returned, some said people treated them poorly because of their scars—scars that didn't exist. Participants believed they had a scar, so they interpreted others' reactions as being a confirmation of their flaw.

In the same way, by believing she was the victim, Bahaar interpreted others' actions and words through that lens. She thought they treated her poorly. So she blamed them based on her interpretation, not their real words and actions.

With this understanding, Bahaar agreed to take the next step and do the Talk Check exercise more consistently. For several weeks, she wrote down the inner conversations as soon as she noticed them. When she later reviewed the pages, she was shocked at how the theater inside her head had portrayed certain scenes, some of which she now knew weren't real. So she continued the Talk Check, using Google Drive to write out her conversations in detail several times a day. She also used

---

7   Rod Dreher, "Ta-Nehisi Coates's Scar," *The American Conservative*, September 12, 2017, https://www.theamericanconservative.com/ta-nehisi-coates-scar/.

Thumb in Fist and felt excited when she saw improvement in her relationship and felt less mental suffering.

After a couple of months, their relationship completely changed, mainly because Bahaar recognized when the internal dialogue started and when she began blaming, and then she stopped herself. She went from blaming him every day to once or twice a week to once a month. And she was much happier as a result.

It's been two years now, and Bahaar recently told me, "He is a really lovely man. His mistakes are no different from mine. We both make them."

In response to our inner conversation, we can also blame ourselves. For months, I had been asking my wife to hang the car keys near the entrance—rather than keeping them in her purse. But she kept putting them in her purse, forcing me to go search for them.

Then one day recently, I was in a rush. I quickly packed my bags and caught a taxi to the airport. While I was waiting for my flight, my wife called. "I cannot find the car keys."

All of a sudden it hit me: the keys were in my bag. I had not followed my own advice about hanging the keys by the entrance.

When I realized what had happened, I felt terrible. My natural reaction was to blame myself: *How could you do that? How could you forget to leave the keys? You have been telling her to leave the keys by the entry, but you didn't do it yourself.*

Years ago, this negative self-talk would have continued for days. Because I had been training my inner voice, however, I used the Talk Check exercise on the airplane. I wrote out my self-chat. This gave me space to consider a way to solve the problem: I used DHL Express to send the key from Berlin to Frankfurt. Sure, it was expensive, but my partner had the key in eight to twelve hours.

Using the exercises to come up with a compensation plan is much more effective than blaming ourselves, which offers no solution to the trouble we make. The exercises also train us to manage our self-talk and decrease the probability of repeating the same mistakes. However, these exercises alone are not *the* solution, nor are the Not to Dos. They all work together in the process of converting confusion into clarity.

When we start blaming, we also open the door to fears. In this case, I feared how others would judge me. Because my wife could not get into the car, she had to share the story with others to explain why she had to cancel her plans. I specifically worried about her mother's reaction: *What's her mother going to think of you? You're an international businessman, flying to a great summit and going off to work on blockchain, but you can't even remember to leave the car keys! What a contradiction! Shameful!*

These fears—in this case, my fear of judgment—waste our time, destroy our focus, and lead to other fears. But they don't get us back to the okay situation. They don't solve the current problem or help us avoid this situation in the future. (More on fears later in the chapter.)

Stop blaming yourself and others; it doesn't work. It doesn't bring you back to peace and calm, it doesn't give you a way to avoid repeating the action in the future, and it doesn't resolve the current issue.

2. DON'T TRICK YOURSELF

When we completely agree with the messages from our Roommate, we can easily trick ourselves into believing lies or half-truths about a situation. Felix, for example, agreed that Ben was wrong for insulting him and his religion. Plus, other people agreed that Ben was wrong. As a result, Felix struggled to see how his Roommate might be offering bad advice. He tricked himself into believing he would benefit from gossiping about Ben and holding on to his grudge.

Even when we are not in full agreement with our Roommate and challenge the voice in our head, we may find reasons to justify our behavior. On some level, we may want to criticize, blame, or gossip because it makes us feel better. Whether we agree with our Roommate or not, the solution to tricking ourselves is the same: find the inner conversation and understand why we are feeling threatened. Then we can tell ourselves the truth: blaming, judging, and other Not to Dos will not get us back to okay.

Many people find the Thumb in Fist exercise most beneficial when working on tricking themselves. It quickly reminds them, *Hey, your Roommate is talking, but you don't need to protect yourself here. Nothing is threatening you—not your partner, boss, or friend.*

When I notice that I am tricking myself by ignoring parts of the truth that have no benefits for me, I write down the whole story, even if I find the details uncomfortable or unpleasant. In one case, I had entered into an investment agreement with someone who then lodged an unofficial complaint against me. We didn't go to court, but we did use a moderator.

At first, I tricked myself into believing I had done nothing wrong. My inner conversation before meeting with the moderator went something like this:

Roommate: It is not in the agreement.

Me: No! There are enough reasons to stop this agreement.

Roommate: Where is it in the agreement?

Me: It's not necessary to be in the agreement!

After meeting with the moderator, I immediately saw how I had been tricking myself. I confessed my fault, and the conflict was quickly resolved.

What if I had not found my fault? What if I had continued telling myself I was right to protect myself as I had? I would have hired a lawyer and gone to court—even though my fault was readily apparent. In the same situation six years ago, before entering serious training, this is exactly what happened. My good friend and I had run a fantastic business together, but we had a disagreement. I believed I was right and refused any conversation with my friend. The extended disputes led to bad results for both of us: we sabotaged our relationship, ruined our credit among people who knew about the conflict, and missed out on money that could have been earned from that business.

Think of how many times people sue each other. How many of these cases could be resolved outside the court if people learned to stop tricking themselves? How many political leaders could avoid making bad decisions? So much pain could be bypassed if humans learned to implement these exercises and stop deceiving themselves.

FEARS

At this level of training, people know the problem: they are reacting to an inner conversation and putting up their guard, which is causing them to act in unhelpful ways. People can see their responses in the conversations they have written down. With this understanding, they are ready to understand the fears that lie behind their reactions.

In our mind, we often jump between thoughts, concerns,

and fears. Thoughts are necessary for everyday life: planning, deciding, giving advice, and so on. We often move from thought to thought very quickly, from thinking about family members to vacation plans to work projects to colleagues. Sometimes these thoughts become concerns: we wonder how our child is doing on his math test or if the project will function as planned. In some cases, these concerns turn into fears: mental suffering about something out of our control that may not even happen. If you leave fears unaddressed, they will grow stronger. Any repetition makes something stronger.

The thoughts-concerns-fears triangle is a picture of how we often mix these three together, resulting in confusion. Healthy thoughts can easily tip into concerns and then into fears. A guy might have an excellent business idea, but if he entertains too many doubts and "what ifs," he might get bogged down in fears and never take the first step. A mother is right to be concerned for her children's well-being and future, but her concern can tip into a fear that pushes her to act or react in ways that are not best for her children. For example, if a mother asks her children not to close or lock the door to their rooms but doesn't clearly explain why, she makes her children confused regarding their privacy. They have heard their privacy is important, but this doesn't appear to be the case. Because her actions are not bad or evil, the mother likely thinks they are valid and reasonable, that she is doing a service for her children even if they don't see it.

The mother may have a genuine concern: if something happened and the children needed help, she wouldn't be able to get in if the door was locked. The children may hurt themselves by misusing their privacy to watch movies inappropriate for their age. But if she is acting out of fear, she probably won't be able to clarify the reasons for her request.

If you find yourself confused at what is going on inside your head, remember the foundational Not to Do: Don't react. Ask yourself, *Is this a valid concern? Or have I slipped into fear?*

Fears and reactions run in an infinite loop. Fear of failure, for example, starts in childhood. We leave the conversation running because no one teaches us how to consider our Roommate—this inner voice that is part of us but not all of us. So the conversation keeps running, we continue reacting, and the fears persist and grow. We hurt people along the way because our input-process-output mechanism is faulty.

We procrastinate in response to a fear of failure: if we don't act, we can't fail. Then we wonder why we have procrastinated again, especially after we promised ourselves that we wouldn't. We lack clarity about our actions and reactions. When we learn to recognize the conversation, we can see when we've procrastinated and understand why we've done it, and then work on a solution.

Fear can also cause us to fool ourselves and others. Have you heard yourself or someone else say things like "So, what?" or "Life's too short"? These statements are sometimes shared for show, as a way to impress others and hide the fear we're feeling inside. We pretend that something isn't important or that we don't care what others say or what happens, when inside we feel quite different. These fears can cause us to make poor decisions in our relationships. We might flee from a relationship because we don't want to work through complex issues, or we might stay in an association longer than we should. Fears can also block the flow of energy and keep us from seeing possibilities for growth and service, and from receiving blessings in our relationships and careers.

In Appendix C, I list 10+1 Fears that many people experience. These fears get mixed up in the inner conversation, and our Roommate uses them to justify actions to get back to okay.

Fears come out when we write out those conversations. We may not see them at first, but when we begin analyzing our self-talk, we start to spot them.

REAL CHANGE

Several years ago, I booked a hotel room for a business trip. When I arrived, I found a long line to check in. I ended up waiting around thirty minutes. As I stood there, my Roommate started talking: "That seems unacceptable since you already paid a lot for the room."

I didn't engage at that point, but my mind was primed for conversation. When I finally arrived at my room, I found it quite cold. My Roommate started again: "See, that is not right. You paid too much to have this happen."

"It's okay," I responded in my head. "I'll look for some blankets."

The final straw came when I ordered dinner, and it arrived more than an hour later. "Now you need to do something!"

My response was natural. Anyone might have been frustrated at these experiences at the hotel. However, I made it worse because all day, I talked to myself and everyone around me about this situation. I justified my reaction with comments like "I'm not a fool to pay such an amount and then find a long line, a cold room, and poor service."

Like Felix, I completely agreed with my Roommate in this case. I thought I was right to blame the hotel staff, so I continued doing so for the next few days. However, this self-talk did not improve the quality of my stay. I blamed the employees, but they weren't directly responsible for the conditions, so blaming them didn't help at all.

After I returned home, I emailed the hotel manager and

received a partial refund. If I had stopped blaming the hotel staff during my stay, I could have made space to think of this solution while I was still at the hotel. Then I could have enjoyed the 80 percent of my experience that was pleasant. But my mind back then was stuck in reacting, and holding on to the negative side of the situation prevented me from seeing any positives. I hadn't yet learned how to manage my internal dialogue.

Today, I would not have the same response and would not feel the need to release my discomfort through blaming. I have also learned not to think in binary ways: good or bad, pleasant or horrible. At the time, I could not see the positive aspects of my hotel stay because I was so focused on the negative. I call this the "destructive binary option of thinking." When we let our Roommate run, we can easily get sucked into this mindset.

The same is true in my relationships. Several years ago, I consistently put up my guard when I sensed someone was disturbing my comfort zone. I took certain comments very personally and felt the need to defend myself. Today, I am aware of when the conversation begins. I understand that my Roommate is seeking to protect me and that I am reacting in an effort to get myself back to okay. Because I notice the self-talk is happening, I can manage it using these techniques, and thus I don't sabotage my relationships. Instead of reacting, blaming, and getting angry, I am now calm. I am more empathetic.

However, I still need to use the exercises and remember the Not to Dos. This is a dynamic process that requires continual practice, and managing is not the end. After we learn to manage our self-talk, we're ready to move on to Level 5: training our inner voice so that our mind engages in inner conversations that focus on true service of others and our world.

EXERCISES

Keep using the exercises discussed in the previous chapters, especially the Talk Check. In addition, use the following tools to help you practice the Not to Dos and manage your inner voice.

Perspectives
To better manage the conversation and our reaction to it, we can remind ourselves to take different perspectives. So far, we have mainly focused on what I call Perspective 0, or Inner: checking what is going on inside our mind. But gaining this perspective is not enough. We also need to see what is going on around us.

First, we need to look at ourselves from the outside, or Perspective 1. This is the Mirroring exercise from Chapter 3: imagine watching yourself as you drive, sit in a meeting, talk to your partner, work at your desk, and so on. To practice Mirroring in an advanced way, you can set up a camera to record yourself for days, weeks, or longer. Put it in a place where you have frequent conversations so that you can go back and observe yourself interacting with other people. Many people find great humor the first time they watch themselves from the outside, especially when they watch themselves in two- or three-times mode. They can see more clearly how they are confused in different situations.

Watching yourself on video can be a real eye-opener. You might think you're managing the situation well, but when you actually observe yourself, you can tell by that tight smile and high-pitched tone that you are not. You can see how you are confused. In everyday situations, remind yourself of how you appeared on video and consider whether you might be doing the same in this discussion or meeting.

Here's how you might use Mirroring, or Perspective 1, in a situation where you feel uncomfortable, for example, a family discussion about a controversial topic that people expect you to comment on. The first step is always to look inside (Perspective 0). Ask yourself, *Am I feeling stressed? Am I anxious? Have I been pushed out of my comfort zone?* Being aware that you are confused already takes you one step closer to clarity. Next, use Mirroring to consider what other people see. Pretend you're watching a movie in which you are a character. What is your body language? What are your facial expressions? How are you interacting with the other characters? This quick check can help you see whether your inner confusion and discomfort are coming out in your words and behaviors. If you can tell you are confused, remember the foundational Not to Do: don't act or react.

In addition to taking Inner and Outer Perspectives, we can take a wider view of the whole situation. Perspective 2, or Situational, involves seeing yourself in relation to everything else in the scene—people, nature, animals, photos on the walls, music playing in the background, and so on. It captures others' reactions to your yelling, laughing, or talking, as well as your actions themselves. In addition, you can consider previous situations where you felt similar emotions and confusion, as these might impact your current state of mind.

In the same example of an uncomfortable family discussion, you might look around at the other "actors" in this movie. How are they responding to you and one another? You also might think of past family discussions. How did those play out? Did something happen the last time that is causing you to feel more cautious now? Finally, in this situation, do you have a commitment to respond at all or in a certain way? What are the responsibilities of the other characters? Considering all these aspects of the whole situation can put your role in perspective. It's most likely not all about you, so you can relax. There isn't really a threat to your well-being.

Perspective 3, or Out of Situation, gives us a view of the environment beyond the immediate situation. This allows us to see, for example, that our conversation or meeting is not the only one happening in a living room or office. In fact, similar conversations and meetings happen in buildings and rooms like ours all over the region and worldwide.

In the family discussion example, you might remember that other families have uncomfortable conversations all the time. People might even be having one right now, down the block or across town. In comparison, your dispute is not unique or overly stressful. Remembering this can enable you to remain calm and consider a proper response.

Most people, including me, learn and practice these four Perspectives in order, step by step. Anytime you feel offended or upset in a meeting or discussion, you can walk yourself through each Perspective to understand what's going on inside and outside, and how the atmosphere or past experiences are impacting you. You can also remind yourself that this situation is not unique and could be occurring all over the state or country at that very moment.

In Chapter 5, we will discuss two more Perspectives: Historical and Universal.

Sky Check
To remind yourself of the relative importance of any conversation, you can do a Sky Check. Think about the size of the

sky in relation to everything on the planet. It's bigger than the mountains, trees, and streams, and it's certainly much greater than us humans and our individual conversations. The sky is unlimited. It has no end.

When you realize your Roommate is speaking and you find yourself confused or stressed, look up into the sky. Remind yourself that in comparison, this meeting or argument, whether internal or external, is nothing.

I highly recommend doing the Sky Check every now and then, even when you're not feeling confused. While driving or walking down the street, look up into the vast sky overhead. This will keep the relative size of your life and difficulties in perspective.

Nonlogical Repetitive Actions
If you have done the Talk Check, then you have probably learned how difficult it is to stop your inner talk once it begins. You might even feel like you can't control your brain. But this is not true. You are in control. You are the one who makes decisions about what to do and when.

To reinforce that you are in control, you can perform a nonlogical action—an action that is not matched to your daily routines or habits. These actions enable you to consciously shake yourself out of the looping self-talk or negative Not to Do. They serve as reminders that you control how and when you get back to the okay situation, not your Roommate.

Here are a few examples of nonlogical actions people take whenever they find themselves in a harmful internal conversation or performing one of the Not to Dos:

- One trainee prays or meditates for five minutes. If possible, he stops what he's doing and meditates right when it happens. If he's in the middle of a meeting or dinner with family or friends, for example, he makes a mental note and then meditates once possible. When he meditates, he pictures a beautiful nature setting and reminds himself that there is no threat.
- One friend takes cold showers. Again, he makes a mental note when the self-talk or blaming happens and then takes the cold shower when he gets home.
- Another trainee pays a certain amount to a charity in her neighborhood every time she blames someone.
- Whenever I engage in a Not to Do, I call or text someone I would prefer to avoid contacting because we had an argument or we are no longer close. Or I clean the alley near my house. During one period, I had a very clean alley!

It's essential to remember that these aren't punishments. They are deliberate choices that serve as reminders that you are in control of your brain. The goal is to decrease the times you perform a Not to Do or get stuck in harmful self-talk.

Chapter 5

SHOULD I LIFT MY FELLOW CRABS?

AFTER SIX MONTHS OF CCC TRAINING, MINDA FELT confident about managing her inner voice—so confident that she stopped doing the exercises. This was a mistake. As with chess or physical fitness, we maintain skills in managing our Roommate through consistent practice.

Minda called me one day and shared that she had faced a series of serious challenges in her romantic partnership. Finally, she asked her partner to leave. "Eric lives on a lower level than me," she explained. "I asked him to behave at my level, but he cannot lift himself up."

But asking her partner to leave didn't help. Minda loved Eric and regretted her decision. She struggled mentally and found herself blaming her partner and others, the same as she had in the past.

Why did Minda become confused again? The problem wasn't her partner. The problem was that she stopped doing the exercises. Because she had succeeded in managing her inner voice and working on most of the Not to Dos, Minda viewed herself as advanced. She looked at the Talk Check, Mirroring, and other exercises as something for beginners.

The only way to progress through this training and build strong, joyful relationships is to continue with the exercises every day. Life is full of challenging experiences. We may successfully manage our inner voice in some cases and then suddenly face a situation where we become anxious and confused. I have been doing this training for seven years, and I still put my thumb in my fist and remind myself to pause and not react.

Only through continuous training can we advance to the next level: service. In Chapter 4, I shared a story about blaming the hotel staff for all of the problems with my stay. At that point, I had been working on CCC training for several years, but I still became confused in that situation and reacted poorly. In the years that followed, however, I became more serious. I managed my Roommate more consistently. I practiced the Not to Dos. And finally, I reached Level 5. My inner voice is now trained to the place where I have a lot of mental space to truly serve others, which is the highest favor I can do for myself too. I see myself as a creature with basic needs that must be met before I am able to pursue my higher needs of self-actualization. In this place, I have the inner space and creativity to serve my colleagues, family members, and friends. I even returned to that same hotel to offer the training program to help the bellhops, housekeepers, waiters and waitresses, and front desk personnel serve their guests more effectively.

In this chapter, we'll discuss the exercises and Not to Dos that are especially helpful in advancing to this level. The ultimate goal is to open space within so our energy flows freely.

Doing so allows us to truly serve—not out of selfish motives but out of empathy and a desire to empower others.

TRAINING FOR SERVICE

To experience true self-improvement and service to others, we have to get to the root: the confusion that results from the faulty input-process-output cycle.

To get to the root, we must understand what is going on inside our head. Always! We need to be mindful that our brain commands our thoughts, words, and deeds. It has a series of tools to protect us and is always looking for the next need to satisfy. With this understanding, we can more readily recognize the inner chatter and remind ourselves, *Ah, this is my Roommate trying to protect me. There's no real threat here.* This is the starting place for not only stopping negative behaviors but beginning positive ones.

It doesn't matter how talented, skilled, or intelligent we are—we all suffer from faulty processing. We all need to train our inner voice to become clear, kind, and empathetic people who serve others and build strong and joyful relationships.

As Minda learned, reaching the "high road" in our attitudes and reactions is not like passing an exam and putting away the books afterward. We have to keep studying. Improving our mental health and living with inner calm takes continual time, effort, and energy. All of the exercises are helpful in this ongoing training, but at Level 5, trainees find that the Perspectives exercise, in particular, frees space for true service.

PERSPECTIVES

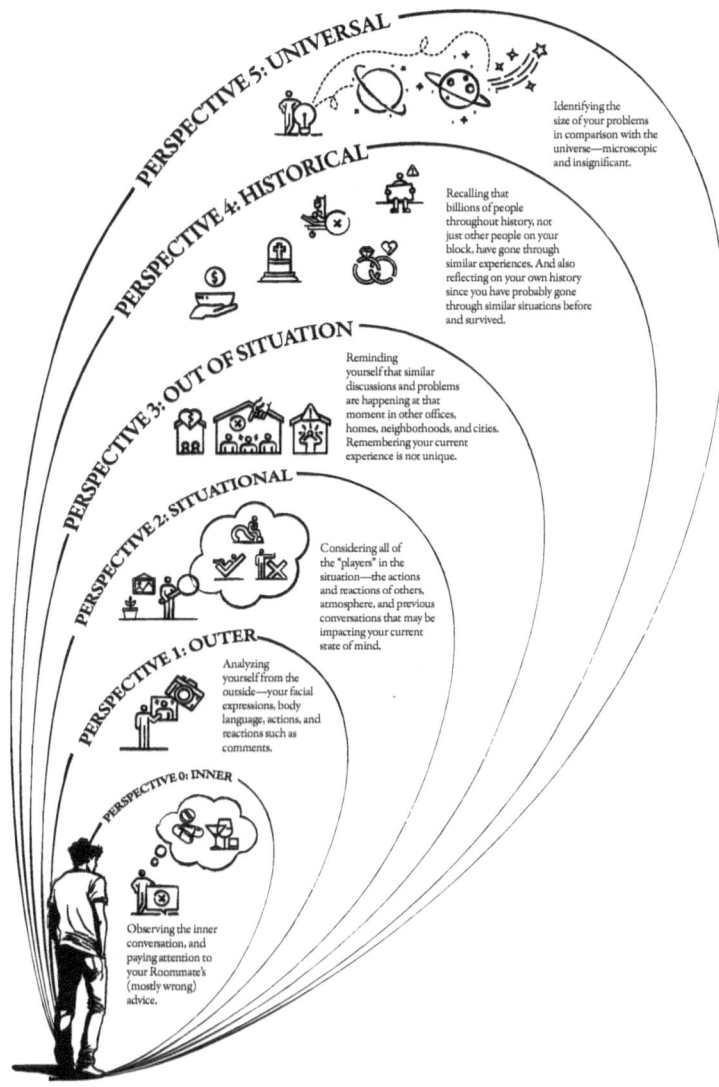

PERSPECTIVE 5: UNIVERSAL — Identifying the size of your problems in comparison with the universe—microscopic and insignificant.

PERSPECTIVE 4: HISTORICAL — Recalling that billions of people throughout history, not just other people on your block, have gone through similar experiences. And also reflecting on your own history since you have probably gone through similar situations before and survived.

PERSPECTIVE 3: OUT OF SITUATION — Reminding yourself that similar discussions and problems are happening at that moment in other offices, homes, neighborhoods, and cities. Remembering your current experience is not unique.

PERSPECTIVE 2: SITUATIONAL — Considering all of the "players" in the situation—the actions and reactions of others, atmosphere, and previous conversations that may be impacting your current state of mind.

PERSPECTIVE 1: OUTER — Analyzing yourself from the outside—your facial expressions, body language, actions, and reactions such as comments.

PERSPECTIVE 0: INNER — Observing the inner conversation, and paying attention to your Roommate's (mostly wrong) advice.

As you learned in the exercises section of Chapter 4, taking diverse perspectives allows us to better manage our internal self-talk and our reaction to it. Looking at situations from all sides reminds us of the relative size and importance of the current event, which can help us discern whether there is a threat and whether we need to protect ourselves in the ways our Roommate is recommending.

So far, we've discussed four Perspectives:

- *Perspective 0: Inner.* Observing the inner conversation and paying attention to your Roommate's (mostly wrong) advice.
- *Perspective 1: Outer.* Analyzing yourself from the outside—your facial expressions, body language, actions, and reactions such as comments.
- *Perspective 2: Situational.* Considering all of the "players" in the situation—the actions and reactions of others, atmosphere, and previous conversations that may be impacting your current state of mind.
- *Perspective 3: Out of Situation.* Reminding yourself that similar discussions and problems are happening at that moment in other offices, homes, neighborhoods, and cities. Remembering your current experience is not unique.

Here are two more Perspectives that are especially helpful in training our mind so we have mental space for empathy and true service.

- *Perspective 4: Historical.* Recalling that billions of people throughout history, not just other people on your block, have gone through similar experiences. And also reflecting on your own history since you have probably gone through similar situations before and survived.

- *Perspective 5: Universal.* Identifying the size of your problems in comparison with the universe—microscopic and insignificant.

If we view ourselves as creatures in an infinite universe among billions of other creatures, both living and dead, we are better able to keep our problems, relationships, possessions, and experiences in their proper place. Our natural way, however, is to attach ourselves to issues, people, belongings, and situations because they are so present and closely involved in our daily lives. And as a result, our mind is consumed with chatter about these things, so we can't notice the needs of the environment, our planet, and people beyond our close circle of family and friends. We don't have room to consider what is going on around us. If we don't pay attention and observe, we can't have empathy and serve.

To explore the enormous blessings and possibilities in the world, we must make space for them and then dig into them. Centuries ago, people didn't believe our voices could be transmitted through wires. Before the telephone became a reality and changed our world, people laughed at the concept. Decades ago, they did the same with the idea of video calls, which have now transformed how businesses and individuals do work and stay connected. These inventions, which we may think of as acts of service, came about because brave and hard-working people freed space inside their heads to explore the universe's possibilities to benefit others.

Think of it this way: If we put our relationships, problems, possessions, and experiences on a plate, we can see them all. They are separated by space. But, if we start losing perspective on their relative size and importance, they grow in our mind. They clump together, blocking out the spaces in between. To engage in true service, we must maintain perspectives. We need to separate those things on our plate so they don't clump together. This enables us to see needs, have empathy, and come up with creative ways to serve and empower others.

Several years ago, I watched a TV clip about a woman who found a six-month-old baby in a box in Iraq during the US invasion. She took him home and raised him as her own son. When asked about her act of service, the mom shared that she is just a "tiny creature" doing good in the world. Her life experiences up to that point in Iraq prepared her for this much greater act of service. She had the proper perspective on herself and her place in the world, and it freed her to make a life-changing difference in this boy's life. It also prompted her to consider other ways she could offer such genuine service.

NOT TO DOS

In addition to the Perspectives exercise, at Level 5, we dive into more Not to Dos—actions that disrupt our calm and negatively impact our relationships with others. It's not enough to read about these Not to Dos or to stop doing one of these actions every now and then. To level up to serving others, we need to become proficient in stopping them consistently.

When we catch ourselves blaming, judging, or playing with the rubbish, we need to stop and ask ourselves why we're acting in that way. What inner conversation has caused us to react? Only with this continual awareness will we achieve real change in ourselves and in our relationships.

We'll highlight three more Not to Dos here (for the first three, see Chapter 4). The rest are listed in Appendix B.

3. Don't Keep the Rubbish

In Chapter 4, I introduced the fears triangle of thoughts-concerns-fears. When our thoughts and concerns turn into fears, they become rubbish that's hard to get rid of. We play with it, turn it over in our mind, and obsess over it. If someone were to ask us if playing with the rubbish is worth it, we would say no. But we still continue.

Why? The answer is always *protection*. From childhood, our family, school, and social systems have sent us a clear message: *Watch yourself. Look out for yourself.* By the time we are adults, our mental and physical systems, led by the brain, are well trained in this regard. However, our protective Roommate is not skilled at classifying or categorizing threats. For example, it does not adequately warn us about obvious threats like the dangers of eating fast food or drinking too much alcohol, though both can have serious consequences for our health. But our Roommate is easily triggered when someone insults us. Immediately our guard goes up, even though those insults pose no real threat to our well-being.

How often does our Roommate protect us from real danger? Not very often. Most of the time, our inner voice puts up a guard and offers advice when we don't really need protection. If we don't recognize what's happening, we start playing with the rubbish. We spend a lot of time and energy worrying about something that really isn't a threat.

Most of us recognize the rubbish and know when we are playing with it. In very rare cases, however, we might be truly confused about whether an issue is rubbish or something that does need further consideration. For example, a friend shares that she is self-harming and needs your help, but she also tells you to keep this information secret. You might struggle to know what to do. Even still, you should not fixate on the issue or try to solve it yourself. You can consult an expert or available resources, talk to your friend, help her come up with a solution, and then put the problem out of your head. Playing with that issue longer than necessary is unhelpful. It wastes time, occupies inside space, and uses up energy that can be used elsewhere.

You may think you don't hold on to much rubbish. When you start writing down your inner conversations, you will probably be surprised at how often it happens. You may also be surprised at how much anger, envy, jealousy, and even hate you hold inside as a result of the rubbish. These negative emotions can also affect you physically. To protect your mental and physical health, you must remind yourself to let it go. Let go of the grudges, fears, and anxieties. You don't need to defend yourself when insulted, criticized, or blamed. When people act this way, they are trying to release their own discomfort. You mustn't let their internal conversations affect your well-being.

4. Don't Pin Your Feelings to External Factors

When we are pushed outside our comfort zone, we often try to make ourselves feel okay by doing things that make us feel good. For example, we might go for a run or go shopping because those experiences have made us happy in the past. In this sense, we pin our feelings of okayness to events and activities outside of ourselves.

From childhood, we have learned to associate feelings with external factors. Think of all the parties and celebrations we attended, and the happiness that came from them. Our brain has been conditioned to expect the return of these good times to make us joyful.

But what happens when those good times don't return? What happens when we are in circumstances that are the exact opposite of a celebration—a cancer diagnosis, for example, bankruptcy, or the burglary of our home? Then we find it very difficult to be happy.

When we pin our feelings to events and circumstances, we make ourselves suffer mentally and sometimes physically. When a loved one dies or when we consider terrible situations in the world, such as poverty and child abuse, we feel heartbroken. We mourn. And that's a natural response. But if we train ourselves to be okay even when everything is not okay, we don't allow that sadness to consume us. We will be able to find joy, happiness, and other positive feelings apart from that awful situation. If we can keep parts of our mind free, we are able to continue with our work and relationships and still be helpful to others.

Think of the qualified people who arrive at the scenes of earthquakes, fires, and other natural disasters. They have been trained to remain focused and energized, despite the tragic scene. They are free to serve others as a result.

If they allow themselves to succumb to sorrow, they block the flow of energy and impede their service. The lives of others depend on their ability to keep their emotions unpinned from external factors.

We are emotional creatures, and sometimes we need to find release through tears. That's natural. But if we don't learn to convert confusion into clarity, we can become trapped in our sadness. As we practice the Talk Check and other exercises, we can find peace and calm no matter what happens. We can enjoy unconditional happiness.

5. Don't Give Space to Negativity

Our world seems to be getting worse, despite all of the advancements in technology and education. We face personal and societal problems on a daily basis. They reach us through circumstances, conversations, social media, and news outlets, whether at home, in the workplace, or out in the world.

With all of these negative inputs, our thoughts and concerns can easily shift to fears—about the economy, the environment, our children's future, and more. If we allow ourselves to ruminate on these fears, we give space to negativity and leave no room for solutions.

As we change our inner conversations and manage our Roommate's influence, we can limit the time we dwell on the negative. When we stop the Not to Dos, like blaming and playing with the rubbish, we free our hearts and minds to serve others, both nearby and around the world.

THE ULTIMATE GOAL

The first four levels of the CCC training focus on clarifying our inner life: observing our inner self-talk, understanding how it impacts our relationships and mental health, and learning to expertly manage our Roommate so we experience a higher quality of life. When we have helped ourselves this way, we are ready for the ultimate goal: serving others.

Have you ever considered that it is possible to serve in an incorrect way? I knew a kind, highly educated researcher who started collecting cats. Some were strays. Others came from people who could no longer care for them. Frank brought them to his home, where he sheltered and fed them. Soon, the cats began reproducing, and many kittens were born. Caring for the growing number of cats required more time, energy, and money, until it finally became impossible to continue. Frank was forced to distribute the cats to other volunteers who had the resources to look after them.

Although Frank had good intentions, he did not know what he was doing. He had not been trained for this kind of service. He simply decided to serve in a way that interested him. He also thought that a decent, well-educated guy such as himself should serve, so why not serve cats? This is not true service. Frank stayed within his comfort zone. Plus, while he served the animals, he neglected his own basic needs, like having a romantic partner and managing his personal finances.

True service involves meeting the needs of others without concern for our own basic needs because they have already been met in other ways. It involves intentionally pushing ourselves out of our comfort zone. Serving in this manner requires an open heart and mind, which only comes when we learn to manage our inner voice at the highest level. When we consistently stop ourselves from reacting, blaming, pretending, playing with the rubbish, and so on, we create internal space for serving. With the negative self-talk under control, we allow energy to flow through us to others.

Getting to this level takes time and practice. Even after I started CCC training, I still needed to work on my own confusion so that I could serve effectively. This became clear during a self-development training several years ago. As I sat in the meetings, my ego felt threatened. My Roommate began a conversation and convinced me that I needed to speak up to show my intelligence and valuable ideas. So, I shared a lot about myself to impress everyone else in the room. In this situation, I was only serving myself. I wasn't sharing my experiences to benefit my fellow trainees. I was satisfying my own need for validation.

The trainer recognized what I was doing. To get me to shut my mouth and to teach me a lesson about true service, he gave me a job: helping a disabled person with his daily needs, including using the bathroom. For the next four days, I performed this challenging task. By the end, I learned something precious: real service outside my comfort zone is very different from "service" that only satisfies my own basic needs. The latter isn't always harmful, but it doesn't bring us onto the high road of living the way true service does. This kind of empathy and empowerment is only possible when we know how to manage and then train our inner voice and free our mind from rubbish, negativity, and fears.

PREPARING TO BE AN ALCHEMIST

Before I was trained to help others, I used service as a way to satisfy my own needs. I'd spend ten minutes looking at a charity's website and then make a donation, feeling quite good about myself. I stayed well within my comfort zone. I didn't dive into their website or call to verify how they used donations or to discover their real needs.

Now, I view service much differently. I don't give for the sake of giving. I plan. I consider my resources, the needs of the charity or person, and the ways I am capable of helping. I intentionally leave my safe place to figure out the priorities and my contribution. This planning and research requires inner space. It is only possible because I've learned how to harness the chatter in my head.

When I reversed my priorities—from finances, certificates, skills, and business meetings to my mental health—I prospered and flourished. And as my life changed and I converted my inner confusion into clarity, I was free to help change the lives of others.

Now, I am working toward the next level, Alchemist. Here, true servers work together in a decentralized way to transform our world. As more and more people learn to train their inner voice and open space for empathy and empowerment, our cities, states, countries, and planet will change. But it starts with each one of us. We each need to convert confusion into clarity and then reach out to others.

EXERCISES

The best thing I've ever done for my own self-development is serving other people, animals, and nature. That said, I needed to learn how to serve in the right way—as a truly selfless act and not as a way to get attention or praise.

The following exercises, in particular, can support you in opening space for true service.

Perspectives
Now you have learned about all six Perspectives. All six are extremely important in learning to manage our inner voice and create space for serving others.

Learning and practicing these Perspectives is a dynamic process, but most people find it helpful to go through them step by step when a conflict arises. Here's an example: Let's say you get into a heated discussion with your partner and feel offended or think you have been unjustly blamed. In that moment, walk yourself through the Perspectives:

- Look inside: Be aware of what conversation has started. Observe what advice your Roommate is giving you. (Perspective 0, Inner)
- Check yourself: How are you speaking to your partner? What

are your expressions and body language communicating? (Perspective 1, Outer)
- Look at the whole situation: Are you feeling sick or nervous? Are you bringing in data from a previous conversation? What is the atmosphere in the room? (Perspective 2, Situational)
- Look outside the situation: Remember other people in your neighborhood or region might be having this same argument right now. Your situation is not unique. (Perspective 3, Out of Situation)
- Consider history: Remind yourself that billions of people throughout history have probably had a similar discussion. Reflect on your own history as well. You have endured heated discussions before and survived. (Perspective 4, Historical)
- Remember the size of the universe: Remind yourself that in comparison to the universe, this offense is so tiny and insignificant. (Perspective 5, Universal)

The more you practice shifting from one Perspective to the other, the more quickly you will be able to go through each one. When experienced, it usually takes less than thirty seconds to go through all six, manage the chatter, and return to a state of calm. Then you can breathe deeply, give your partner a hug, and even laugh about the situation. Together you will then be able to find the best solution.

Even if the end result is a serious decision, like separating from a partner or disciplining your child, running through these Perspectives will help you make that choice calmly, without hurling insults or hurting yourself and the other person.

Position Change
The Position Change exercise is closely related to Perspectives. Here the exercise is to make a conscious effort to put yourself in

others' shoes—to see situations and conversations from their eyes. When you do, you gain greater understanding of why people act and react as they do, and you experience empathy.

For years, I blamed a guy named Greg for his inappropriate behavior toward his family. He made selfish decisions, spread rumors, and turned his siblings against each other. Then I learned that his father had beaten him daily when he was a boy, and I understood that his behavior was appropriate for someone with such a childhood. When I took this Position Change, my internal conversation shifted, and I stopped reacting whenever he acted inappropriately. As a result, I became aware of his positive qualities, which had been overshadowed by his negative ones.

You can also take this same Position Change with yourself to uncover your own history and the reasons behind your behavior. When you dive into these past experiences and conversations, you discover the mindsets you have adopted and the sources of your natural reactions. Then you can apply the training. You will sense when your Roommate starts pushing you to respond in certain ways, and you can work on stopping those unhelpful behaviors and comments.

Taking this Position Change is essential if you intend to train yourself to selflessly serve others.

Shut Open Eyes
This exercise comes from a Chinese proverb: "One eye open and one eye closed." In every situation, remind yourself to keep your eyes wide open, taking account of what is happening within. The goal is to quickly identify what is useful and throw away what is rubbish.

At the same time, remind yourself to shut your eyes to the problems of others. If you keep your eyes open to these faults and issues, you may start blaming, judging, or playing with the rubbish in your mind. For example, I learned that one of my friends had been disloyal to his partner, who was also my friend. At first, I was very confused. I had to pretend like nothing had happened. Inside, my Roommate gave me all kinds of advice: "You should leave it when it's none of your business." "You should do something. He is hurting himself and his partnership."

This confusion would have continued if I hadn't been in the CCC training. I reminded myself to shut my eyes to my friend's problems. This helped me stop the internal turmoil, and it kept me from sharing hurtful comments with others. With space cleared in my mind, I was able to take helpful actions. I talked directly to my friend and asked him to stop his indiscretion. I also invited him to join the training so he could work on managing his own inner self-talk. He indirectly rejected this invitation when he did not attend, so I stopped going to gatherings my friend or his partner had invited me to. He worried that his partner would find this suspicious and then call me to find out what was wrong. He asked me to be silent if she called, and I refused. Doing so would have been harmful to his partner. A series of pressures ultimately led him to seek therapy. Months later, he attended the training program and found more help.

Note that when others don't yet know about the harm caused by others, as in my friend's betrayal, that doesn't mean the harm doesn't exist. Suppose my friend's partner never discovered his disloyalty. In that case, he still damaged his own mental health. He mistakenly assumed that he was adequately managing these two relationships through a series of lies, but his internal conversations were actually leading him astray.

To take the server role at Level 5, you must learn to shut open eyes. This enables you to do what is most useful for others.

Luck Check

A Luck Check is not about being grateful. It's an exercise to see where we have been lucky rather than unlucky. We tend to focus on when we've missed an opportunity or ended up in an unfortunate situation, and we call this bad luck. But what about all the times we have played soccer without spraining an ankle? What about all the times when we have driven carelessly without getting in an accident? Do we call these situations "good luck"? Not usually. If those situations are not good luck, then times when the opposite happens are not bad luck.

This bad-luck-good-luck language is part of inner conversations. We are creatures of the stories we tell ourselves, and if we believe we have bad luck, we set ourselves up for negative self-talk, blaming, complaining, and more Not to Dos.

Over a series of conversations, my friend told me about his bad luck: all of the other kids were doing well in school, but his son was not. In response, I invited him to do a Luck Check. I reminded him that his son was healthy and strong, while many other children in the world are born with diseases and deformities. Why didn't he see his son's health as good luck?

When you find yourself calling something bad luck, do a Luck Check. Remind yourself of all the times when you have had a positive experience in the same situation. Doing so will open space in your mind and allow your energy to flow so you improve your own relationships and engage in real service.

CONCLUSION

IN MANY WAYS, HUMANKIND HAS BEEN IMPROVING for thousands of years. From establishing schools, universities, and social communities to creating new technology to curing diseases, we have made significant advancements that have improved the quality of life for people across the globe.

Despite these improvements, however, society seems to be getting worse. One could become depressed when considering the long list of examples: global warming, water contamination, poor political decisions that lead to millions of deaths, terrorism, mass shootings, domestic violence, poverty, child abuse, animal abuse, racism, sexual assault—the list goes on. For all of humankind's progress, individual and societal suffering doesn't seem to have decreased at all.

In recent years, people have acknowledged these huge, ongoing problems and have offered a simple solution: we need to "do better." We need to be more kind, stop racism, end domestic abuse, monitor hate speech, and so on.

The problem is that we humans can't simply do better. Just as we can't simply "be ourselves," we can't flip a switch and become compassionate or self-controlled. To become kind, empathetic people who serve others and the world, we have to get to the root. We have to deal with the confusion that results from the faulty input-process-output cycle. Only when we convert confusion into clarity can we truly do better, both as individuals and as a society.

WHERE TO START

Remember, this process all starts by paying attention to the conversation going on inside your head. Your Roommate always stands ready to jump in and protect you by offering "helpful" advice on how to get yourself back to your comfort zone. To become a server who makes a difference in personal relationships and society, you must begin with an awareness of this inner dialogue. Then you can choose to ignore your Roommate's suggestions and respond in a way that betters life for you and others.

Let's review the levels of the CCC training and the key takeaway at each level:

- **Level 1: The Observer.** You will succeed in observing the conversations running in your mind most of the time.
- **Level 2: The Analyzer.** You will be able to analyze the internal chats to determine how they impact your relationships, reputation, and mental health.
- **Level 3: The Distinguisher.** You will be capable of distinguishing the roles in your internal conversations: the listener and decision-maker (you), and the speaker or inner voice (part of you, but not you).
- **Level 4: The Manager.** You will succeed in managing your inner voice so that you make better decisions in your relationships and in general.

- **Level 5: The Server.** You will be in a position to truly serve others because you have learned to train your inner voice.

As stated, moving through these levels is a dynamic process that requires daily practice. The ultimate goal is to become as clear as possible moment by moment so that you improve your own mental health and build strong, joyful relationships. At the beginning of the training sessions, I share a health-wealth-happiness triangle to illustrate what's possible. As we learn to observe, analyze, distinguish, manage, and train, we can enjoy the highest levels in all three aspects: we enjoy a healthy state of mind, we feel wealthy because we don't compare our insides to others' outsides, and we experience unconditional happiness because it isn't pinned to external factors. All of which clears space within so we are free to serve our own higher needs of self-actualization as well as the needs of others and our world.

So, where do you start? Let's get practical.

1. *Pick a tool.* Decide whether you will write in a notebook, on Google Drive, or in another tool. Or use a combination of tools like I do.
2. *Set up your tool.* Divide your writing space into different sections: one for Talk Checks, one for Exercises, one for Not to Dos, and one for Fears. Write out the short version of each Exercise, Not to Do, and Fear, so you have them all in one place.
3. *Start writing.* When you realize a conversation has started, write it down word for word. As you start analyzing your conversations, write down the situation in which they happened as well as your actions and reactions. As you begin applying exercises, write down which ones helped you manage your self-talk and return to a place of calm.

4. *Check yourself.* Each week, gauge your progress by identifying how many times you engaged in one of the Not to Dos. Each quarter, create a more thorough report of how often you engaged in one of the Not to Dos. In these quarterly reports, pay particular attention to the gaps—for example, how much you blame others now and how much it has decreased in the last week, month, and quarter. Also, observe when that number soared, and investigate what incident may have caused it.

As you complete the reports and keep track of your progress, you will probably notice your second quarter is worse than your first. Why? As you move through the training and start watching for more Not to Dos, you will become aware of other areas where you are reacting to your Roommate's input. This is a dynamic process because we are always encountering new situations and conversations where we might be pushed out of our comfort zone. If you continue practicing, however, you will likely find yourself back on track in quarter three and continually improving from there on.

PRACTICAL CHANGE

Practicing the exercises and Not to Dos can positively impact every area of your life: your romantic relationships, your connections with friends and family, your business opportunities, and even your financial situation. Let's consider the last one in particular, as this is such a common struggle. After going through training, many people find that the root of their financial problems is found in their negative mentalities, wrong assumptions, and poorly trained Roommates. Whether they are struggling to pay monthly bills or buy a house or donate to charities, many trainees find they are better able to do so when they stop the most common Not to Dos: reacting, blaming, and playing with the rubbish. When the input-processing-output system is fixed, they see more clearly, make better decisions, and enjoy a more positive financial picture.

People often cite financial struggles as the reason they are not serving: *We need to buy a house. We must pay for our child's education. We have to ensure our financial and situational stability for the rest of our life. Then we can give.* If we can clear up the financial concerns by clarifying our confusion, then we open the way to serve, to do something valuable with no strings attached.

Remember Sam and Bahaar from Chapter 4? After overcoming the challenges that stemmed from Bahaar's blaming, they both continued working hard to advance through the CCC training. They opened space in their minds and hearts for true service. As a result, they began using their SaaS company as a way to give back. They now run free boot camps and accelerator programs for young people and immature companies. They also train their team members to convert confusion into clarity.

Their romantic relationship has also grown profoundly, and they have learned to negotiate conflicts quickly and without blaming or judging. They plan to have a child in the near future.

Was the path to living on this high road challenging for Sam and Bahaar? Yes. But they would tell you that practicing the exercises and eliminating the Not to Dos was completely worth it. They have experienced practical, lasting change in their relationship with one another and with others. You can too.

Appendix A

10+1 EXERCISES

THESE EXERCISES ARE TOOLS YOU CAN USE TO REMIND yourself to observe that something is there—that a conversation is taking place inside your mind. They can also help you find that conversation sooner, distinguish between your Roommate and yourself, and manage the conversation so that it doesn't cause confusion that leads to hurtful words and actions.

As self-talk is a dynamic and ongoing process, you need to use these exercises daily to succeed in observing, analyzing, distinguishing, managing, and training your Roommate. This is the only way to enjoy good mental health, build strong and joyful relationships, and open your mind to true service.

0. TALK CHECK

Write down your inner conversations as soon as you realize they are happening. Write them word for word, including your attempts to stop your Roommate.

If you happen to be in a meeting or another situation where writing is impossible, try to keep the details in mind and write when you can. Some people prefer to record an audio message or video of them speaking the conversation and then write it down later. Others take notes by hand and then rewrite the conversation using a digital tool like Google Sheets when they have a chance. Either way, capture every word of what is being said inside your head.

To observe the conversation consistently, to understand how it impacts you and your relationships, and to start managing it, you have to see what is actually being said in the conversations. That's why the Talk Check exercise is first. It is the foundation for this whole training process. You will continue using Talk Check at every level. You may find this exercise challenging at first, but over time it will become an automatic part of life.

It may help to pick a sign to help you remember to write down the conversation. Some people have placed a small tattoo on their hand or someplace that is easily visible. When they see it, they are reminded to see if the conversation is happening and write it down if it is. Others have used a ring or bracelet, and some set reminders on their smartphones.

1. THUMB IN FIST

Place your thumb inside your fist as a way to (1) remind yourself to check whether a conversation is happening, (2) trace the conversation and distinguish between the voices, and/or (3) notice if you are engaging in a Not to Do.

Thumb in Fist is an easy way to check yourself when you are in meetings, driving, or in any other situation where you need a reminder but cannot stop what you are doing. You might even get into the habit of falling asleep with your thumb in your fist and making sure it is the first thing in the morning. These are the times when your inner voice has time and space to be more talkative.

After you have advanced through the training and learned other exercises, the Thumb in Fist can remind you to maintain perspective (see exercise 5), which can help manage the conversation in the moment and keep you from making poor decisions or saying something hurtful.

This exercise can also remind you to check whether you are judging or blaming others, both of which are reactions to the conversation going on inside your head. (See Appendix B for the full list of Not to Dos.)

2. THREE-SECONDS RULE

Pause for three seconds before starting a new activity or engaging in a new conversation. When you feel stressed or uncomfortable, pause for three seconds before speaking or acting.

We live in a fast-paced world, and it's easy to run on autopilot without paying attention to what is going on. The Three-Seconds Rule allows you to slow down and give yourself time to check what is happening: *Do I feel unsettled? Is a conversation about to start? Is a conversation already going on? Am I judging this person? Do I need to make that comment?* This pause also gives you a chance to remember other exercises and lessons you can use to manage a conversation once it starts.

Joan Didion once said that we tell ourselves stories in order to live. The problem is that our inner voice speaks quickly, and we tell ourselves a lot of stories in a short amount of time. The result is that we are the product of the stories we tell ourselves throughout our lives, and many of those stories are not valid or helpful.

The Three-Seconds Rule gives us a chance to pause this quick stream of words and sentences so we can evaluate what should be given more attention. Even if these faulty stories have helped us in the short term, as Joan Didion suggests, they may confuse us later. Think of all the times you have told yourself a story about your correct decision or reaction in a certain relationship, only to find out later that you were entirely wrong. Does this realization make you confused about how to respond the next time you are in that situation? As mentioned earlier, I thought I was correct in writing an email to those top-level businesspeople, but I later discovered the stories I told myself led me astray, and I missed out on a great opportunity. Afterward, I was confused about how I would manage a similar situation next time.

Without exercises like the Three-Seconds Rule, we remain confused and repeat the same mistakes based on the stories in our head.

3. MIRRORING

(1) Imagine watching yourself as you participate in routine activities: driving, talking to a coworker, and typing at your desk. Check your facial expressions, body language, and tone of voice. (2) Whenever you look in the mirror, check your self-talk.

Mirroring offers a unique opportunity to practice seeing yourself from the outside (Perspective 1). This outer view helps you check your responses and reactions, as well as the inner conversation that is causing them. With this awareness, you are better able to take the next step, managing your self-talk and reactions.

Mirroring also provides an opportunity to observe the way you are talking to yourself. You probably look at yourself in the mirror several times a day. When you do, ask yourself, "Am I insulting myself right now? Am I telling myself stories?" If you have time in that moment, write down what you find. If not, make a mental note.

Most of us check ourselves in the mirror hundreds of times each month, thousands of times each year. Each instance provides a natural opportunity to check our self-talk.

One guy who took the training course decided to put a camera in the bathroom to find out who he really is. At one point, when his relationship with his partner became challenging, Henry talked to himself in the mirror: "You are so timid. You needed to stop this bullying, and you didn't. She has ruined your life, and you should kill her." In this case, the Mirroring exercise captured an intense reaction to his inner conversation, a result of playing with the rubbish.

When Henry viewed this video months later, after he had advanced in the training, he was appalled that he had said such a thing.

Henry is not alone in this regard. We all nurture our self-talk in toxic forms, sometimes without even realizing we have done so until we start writing down our inner conversations.

Along with the Three-Seconds Rule, Mirroring is a chance to take stock of the stories you are telling yourself. Those stories come out in your conversations with others, but in front of the mirror, you can practice a new way of talking to yourself and others—partners, children, relatives, coworkers, and friends.

Some of the advanced trainees use Mirroring to say to their inner voice, "I see you. I know you are trying to protect me." It's a way to take the role of trainer, with the Roommate being the trainee.

4. FIXED SHORT PHRASES

Create powerful, strong phrases from the training and Not to Dos. Repeat these phrases to yourself when a conversation has started and you find yourself confused, or when you realize you are doing a Not to Do.

Repeating short phrases can help you stop the current conversation before you start telling yourself stories and before you say something harmful to others. These phrases can be especially helpful in providing perspective.

Sometimes these short phrases come out of longer conversations we have with ourselves. For example, in a meeting, I sometimes talk to myself like this: "It's just a meeting in a room, nothing compared to the universe. These are just people like me. Do you remember what people are made of? We are here to enjoy life and this meeting. If there is a problem, we will solve it together." I've also developed fixed short phrases based on these thoughts, for example, "Ah, we humans!" This phrase helps me avoid harmful self-talk. With my mind free of negativity, I can enjoy the meeting and look for opportunities to resolve problems and contribute positively to the lives of others.

Phrases can also remind you to be empathetic, to stop blaming others, and to remember truths you have forgotten. They can help you laugh at your negative and incorrect thoughts about potential threats. They can even remind you that you are a creature like everyone else, with similar problems and concerns. With such an understanding, you gain empathy and a sense of responsibility for helping others with their struggles.

In the early levels, keep the phrases simple and focused on being aware of conversations starting. For example, you might begin with "Be careful" or "Pay attention." When you are advanced, you can create many options to support you in the moment, and you can make them more fun. For example, one gentleman used to say "I am flying" to avoid getting stuck in any mental trap, negative talk, or confusing situation like a controversial meeting.

5. PERSPECTIVES

Practice taking various Perspectives to check your actions and reactions, and to remember the relative importance of your problems, conversations, and experiences.

0. *Inner: What's going on inside of me mentally, emotionally, and/or physically?* Before you can devise a plan to manage your inner voice, you have to be aware that you are not okay. Simply being aware that you are confused can change the quality of your actions and reactions. The lessons in this book, especially Chapters 1–4, can help you take this Inner Perspective.
1. *Outer: How do I appear from the outside? What am I doing? How am I interacting with others?* The best way to capture an outside Perspective is through video. Even without video, you can imagine yourself standing or sitting in various positions, watching yourself. Try to do that a hundred times a week and write down the results. If you practice this exercise regularly, you will become skilled in checking your actions and reactions throughout your day.
2. *Situational: What's going on around me? How am I interacting with my whole environment in this situation—nature, animals, and so on—not just other people?* This Perspective expands on the Outer Perspective so that you take in everything in the scene. A speaker, for example, might take in all of the conditions in the conference room: the equipment, attendees' expressions and reactions, movements behind

the curtain, and so on. Taking in the whole situation helps us understand the size of the issue. It's just this one discussion involving these three or ten people in this one room. You don't really need your Roommate's protection here. You don't have to react.

3. *Out of Situation: Where am I among others who are having the same experience in their own home or office? How many others are having the same experience?* This Perspective fills a gap between a specific situation and the larger universe Perspective. Many people live in a similar apartment, house, farm, ranch, or region. If you observe the tensions, problems, arguments, and struggles that stem from where you live and work and remember that others live and work in similar locations, you can better understand that your experiences are common and not to be taken too seriously.

4. *Historical: Am I any different from the other humans who have lived on the earth throughout history?* Understanding that more than 100 billion people have lived on our planet, died, and gone through similar experiences can help you maintain Perspective in current struggles. You might even walk around a cemetery as a reminder that all of those people lived and encountered joys and sorrows just like you. You are not alone or unique in what you experience. You can persevere just like those who have gone before. And like many others in history, you can find real joy in life by training your inner voice and serving others.

5. *Universal: Where am I living in this boundless world? What is the size of that place, and my problem, in comparison to the universe?* Compared to the universe's infinite space, the size of the city or even country in which you live is so small—almost as if it is nothing or nowhere. Maintaining a sense of where you fit in that universe can bring Perspective on the

size of your troubles in relation to the bigger picture—very small and really negligible, even though they seem so huge at times. To remind yourself to take this Perspective, you might put pictures of the universe on your walls or computer screen background.

I have worked on these Perspectives for seven years, and within the last two years, I have learned to hold them all at the same time: I see my inner self-talk, recognize how I interact with all creatures, and understand my place in the universe. As a result, I enjoy a much deeper, richer life. I walk in clarity. I am free to serve the current and future residents of this planet.

6. SKY CHECK

Get in the habit of looking up at the sky—rather than the buildings, cars, clothes, and other limiting aspects of your life—to remember the relative size of your problems.

Like the Universal Perspective, the Sky Check helps you remember the relative importance of our everyday lives. Whether you are walking down the street, driving, or sitting in a meeting, when you find your Roommate has introduced a bothersome conversation, look up! Remember that in comparison with the sky, your problems are quite small even though they can feel so overwhelming.

Some trainees have shared that doing the Sky Check frees their minds of all the little issues and concerns. With this space, they can dream bigger and think of others and their needs.

7. NONLOGICAL REPETITIVE ACTIONS

Regularly perform a nonlogical action—something that isn't matched to your daily routines or habits—to reinforce that you are in control of your brain.

Nonlogical repetitive actions are a reminder that you are the one who makes decisions about what to do and when. You can control how you get yourself back to the okay situation. For example, I used to do two pushups every time I entered my office, and then I did two more every time I left—even if it was just to get a cup of coffee down the hall. There's no inherent value in doing just two pushups; it didn't count as exercise, and it wasn't at all related to my work. But by choosing to do that action several times a day, I reinforced control over my brain and over my ability to get myself back to my comfort zone, without sabotaging my relationships. You can do the same.

I recommend starting with something simple. For example, pick up trash on your street whenever you catch yourself blaming others. Or text someone you've been meaning to text whenever you find yourself keeping the rubbish.

8. POSITION CHANGE

Make a conscious effort to change your position with others—to see situations from their perspective.

This exercise is linked to Perspectives, particularly numbers 1 and 2. When you look at yourself and your interactions with others, you can see their facial expressions and body language, which gives a hint as to what's going on inside. Position Change goes a step deeper. It invites you to take time to think about others' backgrounds, family histories, life experiences, and personalities. If you understand these details, you discover the underlying reason for their actions. You gain empathy and compassion. You might not be so quick to judge or blame.

Taking a Position Change reminds you that there is more to life than your point of view. You gain a new appreciation for others' importance. As you exercise Position Changes with your partner, family members, and others, you will strengthen those relationships because people respond positively when they feel understood and valued.

You can also take this same Position Change with yourself to uncover your own history and the reasons behind your behavior. When you dive into these past experiences and conversations, you discover the mindsets you have adopted and the sources of your natural reactions. Then you can apply the training. You will sense when your Roommate starts pushing you to respond in certain ways, and you can work on stopping those unhelpful behaviors and comments.

9. SHUT OPEN EYES

In every situation, keep your eyes open to what's happening within, and at the same time, keep your eyes shut to others' problems, failures, and shortcomings when possible.

This exercise comes from a Chinese proverb: "One eye open and one eye closed." With open eyes, we stay aware of our internal conversations so that we can keep what is useful and throw away what is rubbish. Still, we stand ready to shut eyes when needed. We can't let others' shortcomings and mistakes disrupt our inner peace. If we keep our eyes open to their problems, we will start blaming, judging, playing with the rubbish, and so on. Our inner voice will push us to react when there is no need to do so, and reacting kills the space for solutions and service. If we are in a position to help when others struggle, we will find it challenging to do so if we only consider their flaws. As Werner Erhard said, give space to their garbage.

10. LUCK CHECK

Focus on the luck you have enjoyed, not where you have been unlucky.

A Luck Check is not about being grateful. It's an exercise to see where you have been lucky rather than unlucky. We tend to focus on when we've missed an opportunity or ended up in a bad situation—for example, when we catch a cold before a vacation or get stuck in traffic. We call these situations bad luck. However, we forget all of the other times we had good luck—when we were healthy on vacation or drove down the highway with no traffic.

One trainee's notebook showed that he didn't write down any examples of good luck, but he regularly wrote about instances of bad luck. He also repeated those bad-luck examples to others. This affected his mindset and self-talk because he gave space to negativity (see Not to Do number 5).

When your internal conversation starts heading in this negative direction, talk to yourself. Remind yourself where you have been lucky. This will be easier if you regularly write down instances when things go well.

Appendix B

10+1 NOT TO DOS

IN ADDITION TO EXERCISES THAT TRAIN US TO TAKE new positive steps, we need techniques to help us stop engaging in harmful behaviors. Though our Roommate might push us to blame or pretend, these behaviors keep us stuck in unhealthy patterns. Most of us engage in Not to Dos on a daily basis, and such habits prevent us from building strong, joyful relationships.

One note about comfort zones: we tend to engage in these Not to Dos when we are pushed out of our comfort zone by an interaction or event. In an effort to feel okay again, we look to external factors to make us happy. We put up our guard and close our hearts and minds. We grasp at straws and resort to trial and error, desperately trying to get back to safety and calm.

This is much different from taking a trip outside your comfort zone for the purpose of personal growth and service to others. In that case, we have a plan. We know why we're sitting with discomfort.

Being outside your comfort zone is not necessarily bad. As you engage in Talk Checks and trace your inner conversations, you will learn the difference.

Here is the complete list of actions and reactions to avoid if you want to stop being a crab.

0. DON'T ACT/REACT

When you find yourself confused, feeling threatened, or unsettled, stop. Don't react. Just pause and recognize the situation for what it is. Be aware that if you rush to respond, your actions and words might be full of mistakes and judgments. To avoid being a crab and pulling down others with your comments, it's best to stop. Say nothing. Use the Three-Seconds Rule to insert a delay before you say or do anything. This pause alone can sweeten your relationships and make you more attractive since you aren't piling on unhelpful or unkind actions and comments.

In most of life's situations when you feel confused, you don't actually need to act or react, even though you will feel like you have to do something. In nearly all of life's situations, whether you're in a conversation with another person or listening to a disturbing news story, you do not need to act or react immediately. If you do, your actions probably won't help, and they might even make things worse.

When you pause, also check the situation. What's going on? What's on your mind? What conversation is running there? What are you telling yourself about the situation? Are you about to make a comment based only on your internal conversation? Are you trying to help based on actual skills you can offer, or are you trying to be seen as sociable, wise, and helpful because your Roommate is pushing you?

After checking the situation, write down the conversation (Talk Check) so that you can really comprehend what happened.

1. DON'T BLAME

As mentioned, our natural response is to protect ourselves—physically, mentally, and emotionally. When we feel threatened or uncomfortable, a mechanism in our brain goes to work to get us back to feeling okay, calm, and safe. A conversation starts. We desperately try to release our feelings of discomfort, most commonly by blaming others or ourselves. It's our natural, unconscious effort to push negative feelings onto someone else.

But it doesn't work. It's like throwing a plate against the wall when you're angry. You may feel better temporarily because you've taken some action to release your feelings, but ultimately it doesn't work. It doesn't bring you back to the okay situation, it doesn't give you a way to not repeat the action in the future, and it doesn't solve the current problem. If you blame a restaurant or bank for poor service, for example, it doesn't solve the current issue. It only feeds your mind with more negativity. And the more you practice such blaming, the harder the habit is to break.

Instead, focus on actions you can take right now and the next time this situation comes up.

2. DON'T TRICK YOURSELF

You have probably heard someone say, "Be honest with yourself!" But how can you be honest when you do the opposite daily? If you know that you are doing something to cope with a difficult situation, then don't pretend otherwise. Admit that you don't know why you're doing it or that you know it's unhealthy. Don't trick yourself.

Sometimes when the inner conversation starts and you begin blaming or reacting in one of the other ways described here, you can try to trick yourself into thinking that you're doing the right thing. Don't do that. Be aware of what you're doing and be honest about why you're doing it: you're trying to get back to okay.

One common trick is to tell yourself you're okay for doing X (blaming, justifying, pretending) because everyone else is doing it. Tricking yourself like this is not healthy. It keeps you from stopping the behaviors that sabotage your relationships, your reputation, and your mental health.

Another common trick is to compare your insides with others' appearance. For example, you may see that someone has bought a Lamborghini and assume that he is very rich, at least much richer than you. Then you start getting down on yourself and your accomplishments or financial status, when you really don't know how you compare with the other person. Your Roommate jumps in and convinces you that your assumptions are correct, so you continue in your negative mindset.

Remember that what you see on social media or in the movies is not the whole truth, so don't compare yourself to the external appearance of those celebrities, professional athletes, friends, and acquaintances. You can cause yourself great mental suffering by falling into this trap.

3. DON'T KEEP THE RUBBISH

In other words, let it go. When you are caught in the spiral of an inner conversation and your attempts to get back to okay are not working, let it go.

When you hold on to grudges or continue blaming, you block the positive energy from flowing, which impacts your romantic partnerships, friendships, family connections, and working relationships, as well as your mental health. Keeping junk in your head takes up space and prevents you from considering the precious people, events, and opportunities around you every day. Playing with the rubbish keeps you from serving others because you have no space to think about them or be aware of their needs. It also keeps you from getting back to okay, which is the very thing your Roommate is trying to do. When you let the rubbish go, however, you allow yourself to return to that place of peace and comfort.

To recognize more quickly when you're keeping rubbish, observe the conversation going on in your head. Use the Perspectives exercise to remind you of the relative importance of any concerns you are holding on to.

4. DON'T PIN YOUR FEELINGS TO EXTERNAL FACTORS

When we feel stressed or anxious, we often try to make ourselves feel better by doing things that make us feel good. For example, we might take a drive or walk along the beach because those experiences have made us happy in the past. In this sense, we pin our feelings of okayness to events and activities outside of ourselves. To advance in our training, we need to learn to be okay in any situation, apart from external factors.

In one TV commercial, a waiter walks up to the table. The person asks for a glass of water.

"Oh, we don't have water right now."

"What?" the person asks indignantly.

"Yes," the waiter responds. "You can go to the restaurant across the street, or you can wait about twenty minutes."

"Twenty minutes?!"

A version of this scene repeats itself two or three times. Then Matt Damon appears on screen and says, "Right now, there are people in Africa who have to walk six hours to get clean water."

Once again: everything is okay when you are okay with everything. These restaurant patrons were not okay when it took twenty minutes to get water because they were used to getting it in one minute. The people in Africa are used to walking six hours. They would be happy if that time were decreased to four or five hours, whereas the restaurant patron would still think that is too long to wait for water.

We think life should be a certain way. In fact, our happiness—our sense of well-being and okayness—depends on life being a certain way. When it's not, our inner conversation starts, and we begin working to get back to safety and calm. If we learn to be okay with everything, we won't react, and we won't need to get back to okay. We'll already be there.

When you pin your feelings to things outside yourself, your happiness goes up and down. You live in a land of confusion. But you can change that. As with your comfort zone, you can intentionally choose happiness and peace, no matter what the circumstance. Such intentional happiness is more robust, profound, and constant. As a result, you are clearer and thus kinder, more empathetic, and more service-oriented.

5. DON'T GIVE SPACE TO NEGATIVITY

In our triangle of thoughts, concerns, and fears, we can easily get the three mixed up. A mother, for example, needs to have *concerns* for her children; these lead her to take certain actions to care for them. This is different from having *fears* about her children's future, which is completely out of her control. Which is also different from having thoughts about her children, and planning for their future. If a mother lets her thoughts about the future turn into fears, she might act in ways that could be harmful to her children.

My research online and with trainees shows that humans tend to receive and share negative news much more than positive. Because we are wired for protection and survival, we have the innate need to safeguard ourselves from threats and dangers. This means we are also on the lookout for negative challenges, not positive or peaceful situations.

The basic truth to remember is don't give space to negativity—your own internal pessimism. As mentioned previously, giving space to other people's negative qualities is quite different.

Within your own mind, you do need to distinguish between fears and concerns. Hold on to concerns, but don't entertain fears as these can keep you in mental anguish. For example, shame is a natural reaction. You can respond by apologizing or making it right. But if you give in to dwelling on and playing with your shame for five hours, then you're giving space to that negativity.

6. DON'T CLOSE YOUR HEART AND MIND

We all have a flow of energy moving through us, but we block it by being closed off in our hearts and minds toward people or circumstances. In doing so, we close ourselves off from new opportunities and ideas. As Michael Singer shares in *The Untethered Soul*, we underestimate the power and extent of our inner energy. We don't believe in its capacity, and so we lock down its potential.

When our inner voice or another person tells us that an individual means us harm, we protect ourselves by closing our hearts and minds. A coworker might say, "Be careful of that guy. He only cares about himself and his position." We might not have had a problem with that guy before; we might actually like the person. Now, however, we are more cautious. We become closed off. That response is automatic—a way to protect ourselves and keep ourselves safe.

I received a phone call from a coworker who had discovered how much money the company had in its bank account. "Our salaries could be so much higher if the company has that much!" the guy exclaimed.

My natural response was to start wondering about this guy: *How did he find out that information? Why did he search for the company bank account in the first place? It's none of his business how much money is in their account.* I also started wondering about the company and whether they were really paying me as much as they could.

If I had continued to play with those negative thoughts, I could have become closed off in my heart and mind toward my coworker, my manager, and the company. Even if I said in my head, *Oh, it's the company's money; they can do what they want,* the conversation would have started. If a manager would have then said, "We don't have money in the budget for raises," I would have doubted him. I may have thought he was lying to me. I would have closed myself off to him because of the information I had.

Don't close off your mind and heart in an attempt to protect yourself. Let your inner energy flow. It is key to enjoying positive results in your own life, your relationships, and your service to others.

7. DON'T CONSIDER PAIN EXOTIC

We humans are not okay with pain. We don't think it should happen to us. When we do experience life's hardships, we're often surprised and wonder, *Why me? Why now?*

The truth is that pain in life is inevitable. Family members get into terrible accidents with long-lasting side effects. Friends suffer from incurable diseases. Loved ones die. If we don't mentally prepare for such events and think they only happen to other people, we will increase our suffering when they do. If we accept that hardship is the norm, we can get ready for it. If we are okay with everything, then we won't see pain as exotic or personal. We won't play with the rubbish or give space to negativity when hardship happens. We will see pain as a natural part of life.

When pain does happen, stay with it. Don't complain. Allow yourself to feel the loss or disappointment and give yourself space to mourn and cry. But don't go to the other extreme and discuss your hardship constantly or engage in poisonous self-talk about what you could have done differently. Remember the other Not to Dos: don't keep the rubbish, don't give space to negativity, don't blame yourself or others.

We often want to time our pain, figure out how long we have to stay with it. This is true even in financial markets. People want to know when the stocks are going to rise. They want to get back to okay. Some people react and panic and sell off when the market plummets, but this is often not the best action (remember the foundational Not to Do: don't act/react).

Remember: pain is not exotic or rare. It is part of life. Everyone experiences it. Thinking otherwise will only compound your suffering when pain happens to you.

8. DON'T UNDERESTIMATE YOUR INNER ENERGY

When you haven't learned to take different Perspectives, especially Universal, you can have difficulty understanding your place in the world. In addition, if you don't have a Perspective of your own worth, you can struggle to estimate your capabilities—your potential. Without these two Perspectives, you can't accurately see your size in any given situation.

In addition, by underestimating your inner energy, you limit the amount that flows through you. Have you ever noticed that when you lose track of time, you don't feel as tired, even though you may have worked long hours? That's because there's a difference between feeling tired and actually being physically tired. Research has shown that when you feel tired, you have probably used less than half of your energy. You feel tired because your brain sees fatigue signs, such as the time of day or how long you've been working, and remembers that in the past, you were tired at this point. Then it sends a command to the body: "You are tired! Time to stop!"

Your brain mechanism, the one working to get you back to okay, causes you to underestimate your inner energy because it wants to find a more comfortable situation. Your Roommate is always looking for ways to protect you. It might suggest that you're exhausted or don't have enough energy to achieve this or that. If we're too tired to try, we avoid "failure" or other uncomfortable feelings.

Believe in yourself. Recognize when your inner voice is presenting false claims that you don't have the energy to do X. Resist the temptation to underestimate your energy. Yes, you need to rest and relax, but you should make intentional decisions to do so, not because your inner voice is pushing you. History is full of people who worked hard and never accepted the suggestion that they didn't have it in them.

9. DON'T SET HAPPINESS EXCLUSIVE TO YOURSELF

As discussed in Not to Do number 4, we often pin emotions such as happiness to outside events. When we are pushed out of our comfort zone, we often try to get back to okay by doing things that make us joyful or satisfied. Often these activities revolve around our own personal happiness and have nothing to do with the happiness of others.

If we define happiness in relation to ourselves only, and don't connect it to other people, fears often come up and destroy our joy. But if we broaden our definition to include others, there are hundreds more opportunities to be happy.

Tony Robbins' yachts are parked along the sixty-meter deck in front of his villa. He enjoys them, but they are not the sole source of his happiness. As he shared in his book *Money: Master the Game*, if a hurricane destroyed every one of his yachts, he would still find happiness in other things: giving away a hundred million meals each year, providing drinking water to three million people every day, and more.

If you find happiness in yourself alone, your inner peace will be disrupted. You set yourself up for swirling self-talk and negativity. But if you find deep pleasure in helping and serving others, you will find clarity and calm within. The depth of your experience of happiness will be far greater.

10. DON'T QUIT

This Not to Do is more of a reminder: Don't stop practicing the exercises! If you really want to live on the high road and enjoy life at the deepest possible level, start with solid volition and never quit!

In the process of learning to manage your inner voice, you will fail many, many times. I don't mean ten or twenty times. I mean hundreds or thousands of times. Remember, the goal is to increase the gaps between blaming, judging, playing with the rubbish, and so on. You will never be able to completely eliminate your Roommate.

Also, remember that you may increase the gap to three days

in one situation where you used to blame constantly, and then find yourself blaming every three hours in another situation. It happens. Our reactions are dependent on the situation.

I guarantee that after you practice these Not to Dos for a few years, the gaps in your reactions will be enormous. I am to the point where I'm surprised when I start blaming because it happens so rarely. You can get there too!

Appendix C

10+1 FEARS

THROUGHOUT OUR LIVES, WE HOLD ON TO MANY TYPES of fears. In this appendix, we focus on the fears that result from the billions of unchecked inner conversations that run through our mind. These fears can be significant barriers to change and improvement. Because we don't address the root cause of our confusion, we don't consider these fears and we don't find out why we aren't progressing at a faster rate.

Many of our fears are based on one bigger fear: how we are seen. We worry about how others view us, whether they are judging us, and so on. To help people get through this fear, some self-help courses encourage people to be themselves—but they don't tell people *how* to do that. That's what we do in the CCC training: through exercises such as Perspectives, we learn to take a full view of ourselves and our place in any situation. If we have this insight, we maintain a proper estimation of our size and the size of our problems, and we won't feel the need to pretend. We will be ourselves.

If we can get to the place where we are okay with who we are, we will be more secure in our relationships and partnerships. We will not create fears by comparing ourselves with others or by worrying about how they see us in comparison with themselves.

In some rare situations, we act without fear. If our child is in the street and a car comes around the corner, we will jump into action, with no fear of consequences or how we are seen. But those cases are rare. Most of the time, we worry about what others think, or feel the need to do something to make ourselves look okay. Our fears move us to blame, judge, and play with the rubbish. Fears compel us to act to try to get back to the okay situation.

We all have basic fears as humans. They start to form when we are very young. Then we grow and start challenging the negativity life brings. We learn what it's like to feel okay, and we learn many coping mechanisms to keep ourselves feeling okay. We try our best to remain happy and content, but other fears arise. Society trains us to pretend, not to dig down to find out what is really happening and why we react the way we do. We can learn so much about our fears by writing down the conversations we have with our Roommate.

O. FEAR OF FAILURE

Based on the Talk Checks I've seen in training, the most common fear is the fear of failure. It is behind pretending, procrastination, justification, blaming, feeling shame, and more. Sometimes it even shows up as a fear of failure for others, for instance, our children.

A woman I know had such a fear of failure that she ruined her children's lives. From the time her kids were young, Paula told them horror stories about failed marriages and worst-case scenarios that happened to others. As they grew older, the children found evidence in the world that what she was saying was true. As a result, none of them married because of this irrational fear of failing in that relationship.

As adults, Paula's children justified these fears, pointing to people who had separated from their partners and suffered as a result. They even warned others to avoid marriage. If you were to ask them about successful partnerships, they would say it's only a matter of time; the couple will break up, or they will stay and suffer. If you were to ask them about older people who have stayed married despite experiencing many ups and downs, they would say those individuals are either pretending to be happy or are the rare exception.

Unlike the other fears, we encounter fear of failure at a young age. At three or four years old, we don't face a fear of fate or poverty. We do face a fear of trying new things and not succeeding. My son is three. When he tries something new and finds it's not possible for him to do it, he feels sad. I am quick to remind him that there's no need to feel bad. He didn't do anything wrong. The task was simply too difficult for someone his age or size.

When we let conversations run in our mind, fears naturally arise. People may achieve significant accomplishments and still fear failure because they let thoughts and concerns turn into fears.

With this foundational fear, the primary concern is how we are seen—not how we really are. However, if we are clear on who we are and what we can do, we will not need to react. Before I started this training, when my business partners asked if something was possible, I would immediately react with "Yes. That can be done." I wanted them to see me as competent and smart. Today, I pause. I use the Three-Seconds Rule and remind myself not to answer immediately. Then I say something like "I'm not sure. I have other tasks on my plate, so I'll have to work on it and let you know if it can be done."

Such a response takes bravery. When we are confused, we don't have the confidence to be this brave. We may not even know what bravery is.

Concern that a project will fail is different from fear of failure. With concern, we may point out that the project is risky and that there are several potential obstacles to success, but we would still initiate the work. We would assess the risks and do our best to mitigate them along the way. Someone with a fear of failure wouldn't begin the project in the first place.

Through the exercises, you learn to observe when your Roommate is telling you stories to keep you "safe." You can learn to recognize when you avoid projects or duties because you fear failure. And you can change your responses so that you open the door to new possibilities.

1. FEAR OF JUDGMENT/CRITICISM

When we react with blame to get back to our comfort zone, we waste a lot of time and energy. Underneath our tendency to blame is a fear of judgment or criticism, as well as a fear of how we are seen and how we may feel later. We react by pushing that judgment or criticism onto others.

I didn't think for one second that I could write a book. Because I have worked to become clear about who I am and what is going on in my mind, I have conquered several fears around carrying out this task. I can distinguish between my voice and my Roommate's voice, so I don't feel unsettled. I don't need to blame or react. I can choose how to respond.

Keeping ourselves open to feedback and criticism, and then investigating if they are based on facts and numbers, is one of the ways we can defeat such a fear.

2. FEAR OF EMBARRASSMENT

Fear of public embarrassment is connected to fear of judgment, but it may also involve a real lack of skills. For example, I have several doctor friends who are highly skilled in medicine. Whenever we get together and they start discussing doctor things, I have nothing to contribute. A fear of embarrassing myself sits in my mind. I usually have something to say when we discuss other topics, but with my doctor friends, I say nothing. They don't ask questions or push me to comment. The fear is all in my head.

Before training my inner voice, this fear led me to blame my friends for talking medicine *again*. I would say things like "Hey! Some are not doctors in the gathering." Now, I do not blame. To enjoy my time with these friends, I use Thumb in Fist to remind myself to check my self-talk, and then I use Perspectives to manage the conversation. I remind myself that we are all insignificant creatures, so small in comparison with the universe. This helps me enjoy the discussion instead of feeling embarrassed. In situations like this, we may not know where our embarrassment comes from. In a sense, it doesn't matter. The answer is the same: after we are aware of our response, we can overcome and finally remove it using exercises such as Perspectives.

When we fear embarrassment, we naturally react by blaming to justify ourselves and make ourselves feel better. But when we do this, we still absorb the negativity. If we are aware of our fears and the suffering we are causing ourselves, we can try to stop these actions by using the exercises.

One young woman suffered from a fear of public embarrassment because she was fat. Emma was comfortable in the workspace because people didn't look at each other that much, and conversations focused on the projects, not other people. But in a party setting, she struggled. She suffered mentally every time she had to attend a function outside of the office, where her coworkers tended to gossip. She feared being compared to others in that public space.

More than skills or certificates, the exercises in this book gave Emma the power to conquer this fear. She let go of the body shame because the internal conversation became clear, and after a while, she came to love herself just as she was. In addition, her clearer mind allowed her to care for her body. Before, negative self-talk left no room for pushing herself to take a beneficial action. With space in her mind for positivity, she felt motivated to work out regularly, which further contributed to her confidence.

3. FEAR OF IMPERFECTION

Whereas fear of embarrassment is based on comparing ourselves with others, fear of imperfection comes from looking at and judging qualities in ourselves.

Many people are afraid of being imperfect—of not being beautiful or physically fit. Social media has made this worse because we are always comparing ourselves to others based on external factors like our looks. Most intellectual people claim they are not affected by social media cruising, but the truth is something else.

This fear comes from not accepting ourselves as we are, so we fear how we are seen by others. We all have imperfections; they are a beautiful part of each of us. However, if we play with our faults as rubbish, they can become harmful, not only to ourselves but to our relationships and our ability to serve others. If we learn to manage our inner voice, we can come to love our imperfections and take steady steps toward improving ourselves without hating where we currently stand.

4. FEAR OF DISEASE AND DEATH

As humans, we have the possibility of suffering mentally as well as physically. If we are suffering mentally, then something is wrong. We've likely mixed up concerns and fears. Concern that leads to action, such as seeing the doctor, is natural and right. But concern that leads to worry, rumination, and mental suffering is actually fear.

Some diseases are genetic, so we worry about inheriting them. We watch our children play in a completely healthy state and still worry about them getting sick or having an accident. We worry about them going to school and what might happen there. If these concerns lead us to suffer, to feel the need to do something to release our discomfort, then they have moved into fears.

With clarity of mind, we can see what is happening and let these fears go. We can stop playing with the rubbish.

5. FEAR OF LOSING SOMETHING PRECIOUS

Losing a family member or romantic partner is painful when it happens, but we can also develop a fear of that loss long before it comes to pass. This fear can be quite destructive, especially for teenagers who can be shortsighted. A high school boy I knew committed suicide after his mother got cancer because he so feared losing her. Her cancer was curable, but he couldn't stop playing with the rubbish once the conversation started. He justified his decision by saying everything was pushing him to kill himself. He felt useless and believed he would miss all of his loved ones soon anyway, so he might as well take matters into his own hands.

Some people think those who struggle with a fear of losing someone or something precious are rare cases or have a genetic mental problem. This is not so. All of us are susceptible to this fear because all of us have cherished loved ones and experiences, and even precious belongings, that we don't want to lose. When we play with this fear, however, we destroy our present moments and miss out on joy.

This fear is especially connected to the Not to Do "Don't Keep the Rubbish." Through exercises and practice, we need to learn to let this fear go.

6. FEAR OF TIME PASSING

This fear is linked to a fear of getting older, of having missed the opportunities that life has presented to us. Regret over what we have not done can run deep. We may have missed an opportunity years ago, and we keep thinking about it. We can't let it go. Playing with it does nothing but make us sick. We can't change the past, and revisiting our regret prevents us from taking action in the present.

Like the fear of losing something precious, this fear can be dangerous, even to the point of committing suicide.

You are not alone in suffering from this fear, but you can defeat it through the exercises and Not to Dos. Take time to trace your inner self-talk to learn if your inner confusion is based on this fear. If you find it there, create a short phrase to repeat to yourself when you experience the fear.

7. FEAR OF COMMITMENT

Fear of commitment can also be considered a fear of challenge or responsibility. For one trainee, this showed up as not wanting to get married. At age thirty, thirty-five, then forty, when a girlfriend asked Pol about getting married, he got upset and blamed her, when her desire was natural. His fear of commitment was the problem. This fear is rooted in fear of failure.

When three different relationships ended, each of the young ladies told Pol that he was terrible because he didn't keep his promises, yet he still pretended to feel happy and lucky. He didn't take their comments seriously. He tricked himself into thinking that what's important is his external appearance, his lifestyle, the fact that people liked him because of his skills, his sense of humor, and so on.

If you don't investigate deep inside yourself to see if you hold this fear of social, partnership, and family commitments, you will sabotage your relationships and reputation.

8. FEAR OF POVERTY

In 2007, Adolf Merckle was the fifth richest man in Germany. *Forbes* magazine estimated his personal worth at more than $9 billion, while his companies' combined turnover was greater than $29 billion. Then Merckle made a poor financial decision, and overnight his financial status dropped dramatically. He was so distraught that he killed himself.[8] Merckle was still worth billions of dollars and owned several giant companies, but in his mind, he was poor.

Fear of poverty is more powerful than you may think.

Like fear of embarrassment, fear of poverty stems from comparing ourselves to others and worrying that we don't match up. It is linked to stories we tell ourselves and then play with over and over. We gather information about others' financial status,

---

8   Cristina von Zeppelin, "German Billionaire Merckle Kills Himself," *Forbes*, January 6, 2009, https://www.forbes.com/2009/01/06/billionaire-merckle-obit-biz-billies-cx_cvz_0106merckleobit.html?sh=e97bbb2316d2.

much of which is irrelevant to our situation (faulty input), and then process it based on the habits of our internal conversations, which leads to faulty output: fear.

If we feel poor, it means we see ourselves as inferior to others. When we encounter signs of others' wealth, our Roommate starts playing with that fear of poverty. To find release, we tell ourselves stories. For example, we might think, "If I had as much money as *that* guy, I would do better. I would make smarter choices. It's bad luck that I don't have that money and he does."

Many people pursue money every day and miss many precious experiences because they are so consumed with becoming poor again or not staying poor or not being rich like others.

9. FEAR OF FATE

Based on our gender, race, genetics, and family history, we gain a deep sense of who we are and what we can accomplish. As a result, we can develop a fear of getting stuck in that place or role. If our ancestors have lived in poor or midlevel conditions, for example, we may fear that our destiny lies in the same, even if we claim something else verbally. If we live in a country that has a history of certain kinds of political policies, we may fear it will always be that way even if we claim that it should be changed. These fears are deeply ingrained so that we cannot easily see them for what they are.

In addition, we can feel bitter about where we were born. People sometimes think that if they had just been born in this country or into that family, things would be different. But this is not true. Family, country, race—these are all external factors, but they are not our real essence. We are not stuck. Our destiny is not determined. We can look within to discover our own personal interests and capabilities, and we can carve our own paths. First, however, we have to address the conversation in our head that tells us something different.

People listen to the news and hear about the many negative things happening in Germany. Their natural response is to react. If they hear that inflation is up to 10 percent, they might say, "Shame on you, Chancellor, for letting this happen!" Blaming like this is natural, but it is not helpful. You are still absorbing the negative, at the same time that you are tricking yourself into thinking yourself to be an intellectual—at least smarter than the person who is a so-called expert.

When we blame and talk negatively about political leaders like this, a fear of fate is the cause. We worry about what will happen to us in this city, state, or country and think we should have been born elsewhere.

This is just another story we tell ourselves. If we are concerned about our neighborhood or city, we should look for ways to help. But only after we have managed our own inner voice so that our service is true and not an effort to satisfy our needs.

10. FEAR OF LOVE

Fear of love appears in various ways: fear of being loved, fear of not being loved, fear of loving someone, or fear of not loving someone. Here we'll consider just one: fear of not being loved.

Just as we can tie our okayness to external events and circumstances, we can also tie it to those we love. When our relationship with our partner or children is okay, then we feel okay. If they are feeling at peace, then we feel at peace. As long as we feel loved, then we feel okay—but as soon as we don't receive enough love, or sense that something is wrong, we lose our sense of peace and calm. Out of fear of not being loved, we sometimes do crazy things to receive that attention and love again.

In this way, we make those we love much more important than appropriate. We make everything in life linked to our partner or children—what they think, what they want, and what they're doing. As parents, we consciously or unconsciously compete for our children's love. This is not healthy.

Remember: everything is okay when we are okay with everything. We don't have to fear not being loved. As we learn to manage our inner voice, we will come to love ourselves. Then we will not have to fear losing the love of others. When we learn to love ourselves, we make space to serve others and receive their love.

ACKNOWLEDGMENTS

I AM ETERNALLY GRATEFUL TO ALL WHO SUPPORTED me in writing my first book:

Very special appreciation to Gail. I couldn't have pulled this off without you and your creative Roommate. You are fabulous!

To Miles, Sophie, Libby, Jane, Rebecca, Prof. Rob, and Dr. Alex. Your guidance was so helpful. You are awesome, mates!

To my wonderful wife, fantastic mom, outstanding dad, remarkable sister, precious family members, and amazing close friends. Thank you so much for supporting me along this writing journey. You are my heart, besties!

To my young son, my "sun," who has given me a reason to be passionate about and dedicated to overcoming the challenges of working on the CCC training and this book. I hope you start living on the high road as soon as possible and serve others throughout your life.

To Sarah, Hooman, Sam, and Mahmoudreza. Many thanks for your companionship on the CCC path and for your feedback on the book. You are so generous, my friends!

To Massi, Farzin, Abbas Jon, JeVon, and Tucker. You inspired me to write this book. You are daring leaders!

And thanks in advance to all who lowered their guard and read my book. I already love you, dudes!

Finally, thanks a bunch, Roommate! You gave me space to harness you, and we have both become servants.

Writing this book was an amazing process, and I greatly appreciate how you all contributed.

ABOUT THE AUTHOR

Thought leader and serial entrepreneur HOOMAN MOTEVALLI is a senior business analyst and in-demand consultant for high-level blockchain and AI software teams. He is the director of HSP Holdings, an IT-based company investing in intelligent blockchain and DAO-Metaverse startups. Motevalli also works to improve the qualities of tech and business teams through his Converting Confusion to Clarity (CCC) training program. He is a macroeconomics expert, holds a BS in Chemical Engineering from Sharif University of Technology, has a master's degree in theater from the Academy of Art University, and is a UEFA soccer coach. Motevalli is currently studying at Stanford University.

Here you will find all the links to Hooman's CCC Training program, official website, and media channels:

https://linktr.ee/hoomanmotevalli

www.ingramcontent.com/pod-product-compliance
Lightning Source LLC
Chambersburg PA
CBHW030526080526
44586CB00011B/333